From Generation to Generation

W9-BPM-934

THE AZRIELI SERIES OF HOLOCAUST SURVIVOR MEMOIRS: PUBLISHED TITLES

From Generation to Generation

Agnes Tomasov

SECOND PRINTING

Copyright © 2012 The Azrieli Foundation and others

The Azrieli Foundation
www.azrielifoundation.org

Cover and book design by Mark Goldstein
Endpaper maps by Martin Gilbert
Inside maps by François Blanc

LIBRARY AND ARCHIVES CANADA CATALOGUING IN PUBLICATION

Tomasov, Agnes, 1930–
    From generation to generation/Agnes Tomasov.

(Azrieli series of Holocaust survivor memoirs; 3)
Description based on Publisher data. This item is not in the LAC collection.
Includes bibliographical references and index.
Summary: Agnes Tomasov's sweeping memoir of life under two totalitarian regimes is an extraordinary tale of courage, love and hope in the face of tragedy.
ISBN-10: 1-897470-19-3. – ISBN-13: 978-1-897470-19-0

1. Tomasov, Agnes, 1930–. 2. Holocaust, Jewish (1939–1945) – Slovakia – Personal narratives. 3. Jewish children in the Holocaust – Slovakia – Biography. 4. Holocaust survivors – Canada – Biography. 5. Slovak Canadians – Biography. I. Azrieli Foundation II. Title. III. Series: Azrieli series of Holocaust survivor memoirs; 3

D804.196.T64 2010   940.53'18092   C2010-904512-2

MIX
From responsible sources
FSC® C004191

PRINTED IN CANADA

The Azrieli Series of Holocaust Survivor Memoirs

Contents

Series Preface:
In their own words. . .

In telling these stories, the writers have liberated themselves. For so many years we did not speak about it, even when we became free people living in a free society. Now, when at last we are writing about what happened to us in this dark period of history, knowing that our stories will be read and live on, it is possible for us to feel truly free. These unique historical documents put a face on what was lost, and allow readers to grasp the enormity of what happened to six million Jews – one story at a time.

David J. Azrieli, C.M., C.Q., M.Arch
Holocaust survivor and founder, The Azrieli Foundation

Since the end of World War II, over 30,000 Jewish Holocaust survivors have immigrated to Canada. Who they are, where they came from, what they experienced and how they built new lives for themselves and their families are important parts of our Canadian heritage. The Azrieli Foundation's Holocaust Survivor Memoirs Program was established to preserve and share the memoirs written by those who survived the twentieth-century Nazi genocide of the Jews of Europe and later made their way to Canada. The program is guided by the conviction that each survivor of the Holocaust has a remarkable story to tell, and that such stories play an important role in education about tolerance and diversity.

Millions of individual stories are lost to us forever. By preserving the stories written by survivors and making them widely available to a broad audience, the Azrieli Series of Holocaust Survivor Memoirs seeks to sustain the memory of all those who perished at the hands of hatred, abetted by indifference and apathy. The personal accounts of those who survived against all odds are as different as the people who wrote them, but all demonstrate the courage, strength, wit and luck that it took to prevail and survive in such terrible adversity. The memoirs are also moving tributes to people – strangers and friends – who risked their lives to help others, and who, through acts of kindness and decency in the darkest of moments, frequently helped the persecuted maintain faith in humanity and courage to endure. These accounts offer inspiration to all, as does the survivors' desire to share their experiences so that new generations can learn from them.

The Holocaust Survivor Memoirs Program collects, archives and publishes these distinctive records and the print editions are available free of charge to libraries, educational institutions and Holocaust-education programs across Canada, and to the general public at Azrieli Foundation educational events. Online editions of the books are available free of charge on our web site, www.azrielifoundation.org.

The Azrieli Foundation would like to express appreciation to the following people for their invaluable efforts in producing this series: Mary Arvanitakis, Josée Bégaud, Florence Buathier, Franklin Carter, Mark Celinscack, Darrel Dickson and Sherry Dodson (Maracle Press), Andrea Geddes Poole, Sir Martin Gilbert, Pascale Goulias-Didiez, Stan Greenspan, Karen Helm, Carson Phillips, Pearl Saban, Jody Spiegel, Erika Tucker, Lise Viens, and Margie Wolfe and Emma Rodgers of Second Story Press.

Introduction

It has been said in jest that what history teaches most is that here and now is better than then and there. For some people, this is not a joke and it is certainly not a joke to Agnes Tomasov. In her boldly honest memoir, *From Generation to Generation*, Agnes shares the story of her life, a life repeatedly buffeted by cruel winds of history. As if to prove that life's struggles are never apportioned equally, Agnes survived the Holocaust, suffered an iron-fisted Communist regime that willfully encouraged antisemitism as state policy, was crushed by the false hope of liberating reform in her homeland and endured the doubts and insecurities that beset those who are forced to begin a new life in a strange land. And in the end, she succeeded. She built a new life for herself and her family, a life secure and sheltered in a land governed by the rule of law.

Agnes tells her story through the eye of memory – memory of events, places and experiences to which she was witness – and memory that to this day, for Agnes, remains as close to her as her own breath. And her memory has not dulled with time – on the contrary, it is as remarkable in its clarity as her memoir is in its candour. At the same time, as with each of us, Agnes's memories are inevitably the stored remembrance of past experience – what she did, heard and saw. As much as she remembers, she cannot describe first-hand what lay beyond her peripheral vision, that is, the larger historical context – international, national and local – within which Agnes's own history unfolded. The broad outline of that history is important to readers of this memoir and this introduction modestly attempts to provide something of that larger historical context. It is offered as a complement to Agnes's own moving story.

If our earlier years are the platform on which we build our adult lives, Agnes's early years are telling. She was born Agnes Grossmann on June 16, 1930, in Bardejov in northeastern Czechoslovakia. Her mother, Katka Kohn Grossmann, died when Agnes was only two years old and she was barely three when her father married a woman who showed Agnes little warmth. Her brother, Ivan, was born a year later in 1934. Although Agnes was close to her brother, she found the greatest comfort in summers spent with her mother's family – her grandparents Zelma and Armin Kohn and her beloved uncles Jozko and Bandi – in Levice, close to the Czechoslovak border with Hungary. In 1938, Agnes spent her last carefree summer with her Levice family. Within a year, Levice would no longer be part of Czechoslovakia; Czechoslovakia would no longer be an independent state, and, in many ways, Agnes's childhood would be over.

Czechoslovakia was cobbled together out of provinces of the former Austro-Hungarian Empire in the aftermath of World War I. The new country enjoyed relative political stability through the 1920s and into the 1930s. This is not to say that Czechoslovakia was problem-free. Particularly difficult were minority ethnic and linguistic divisions. When Czechoslovakia was founded, its population included Czechs and Slovaks as well as large German, Polish and Hungarian-speaking minorities concentrated on Czechoslovakia's borders. While they were citizens of Czechoslovakia, each of these national minority groups harboured irredentist political movements pressing not just for regional language and cultural autonomy, but also for the political transfer of their particular region to what they regarded as their respective national and linguistic homelands – Germany, Hungary and Poland.

This issue of irredentism grew increasingly acute after the Nazis assumed power in Germany in 1933. Nazi policy called for ingathering of peoples and territories Germany claimed were inherently German, areas populated by German *Volk*, and it was a policy put into practice. In 1935, following a local referendum on unification, Germany unilaterally absorbed the Saar region that had been administered under a League of Nations mandate since the end of World War I. A year later, in violation of the Treaty of Versailles that ended World War I, the German military marched into the demilitarized Rhineland and Hitler again "legitimized" the takeover by staging a referendum, this time an after-the-fact referendum. In March 1938, after a series of provocative moves, Hitler sent his troops into his native Austria and announced its annexation to Germany. With Nazi troops securing the seizure, yet another popular referendum was staged to validate the takeover. None of these Nazi moves met with major resistance from either the local populations or censure by the countries that had defeated Germany in World War I.

Hitler next turned his attention to Czechoslovakia. In the name of "reclaiming" Germans into a greater Germany, Hitler demanded that the Sudetenland, with its large ethnic-German minority, be ceded to Germany. The Czechoslovak government would have none of it but in Munich in March 1938, Britain and France, fearing war with Germany and hoping Hitler's expansionist appetite would be satisfied with the Sudetenland, ignored Czechoslovak protests and agreed to the transfer of the Sudetenland and its population to Germany. Poland and Hungary, energized by the German annexation of Czechoslovakian territory, demanded their own border adjustments. In parallel agreements, the Polish and Hungarian ethnic border regions of Czechoslovakia were handed over to Poland and Hungary respectively. Czechoslovakia was shorn of more than one-third of its population and territory. Included in the territory handed over to Hungary was the town of Levice where Agnes spent childhood summers with her mother's family. In the summer of 1938, with the transfer of Levice to Hungary only a few months away, eight-year-old Agnes spent her last happy summer there. She would never see many of her maternal relatives again.

Britain and France had sacrificed Czechoslovakia in the hope of averting another war in Europe. It was a false hope – the carving up of Czechoslovakia did not secure peace. In spite of repeated assurances to the contrary, Hitler was not content with the Sudetenland. In March 1939, Hitler ordered German troops across the Czechoslovak frontier to assume control of what remained of Czechoslovakia. The Nazis partitioned the former Czechoslovak state and the western Czech regions of Bohemia and Moravia were designated a German "Protectorate" under direct German control. Slovakia, where Agnes and her family lived, was declared independent but in reality was little more than a Nazi puppet state. By seizing what remained of Czechoslovakia, Hitler's claim that Germany's territorial ambitions were limited to bringing ethnic Germans and the lands they inhabited into Germany was finally seen to be a lie. Britain and France could no longer turn a blind eye to Hitler's expansionist agenda and pledged to defend Poland in the event it was attacked. That attack was not long in coming. On September 1, 1939, Nazi Germany invaded and quickly conquered Poland. Britain and France declared war on Germany.

The new Nazi-allied government in Slovakia walked a fine line between its need to follow the Nazi lead and its desire to act as an independent state. Turning on Slovakia's Jews and others labelled as enemies of the state served both these ends. Some of those who opposed the Nazi puppet government fled Slovakia or went into hiding. Many more were arrested and eventually murdered. For Agnes and her family, the establishment of a Nazi-allied state in Slovakia meant the imposition of Nazi-like racial laws. As a first measure, Slovakia ejected all Jews from the military and government positions. But the circle of repressive anti-Jewish regulations quickly expanded. In short order Jews were denied access to public amenities, including parks and sporting facilities. Legislation was passed permitting uncontested confiscation of Jewish-owned businesses and property. Jews were even denied the right to drive cars or purchase first or second-class tickets on trains. But far worse was yet to come. On September 9, 1941, the Slovak government bundled its anti-Jewish laws and regulations together into a "Jewish Code" modelled on the 1935 Nazi Nuremberg Laws.

The Nuremberg Laws, passed into law by the German Reichstag in the autumn of 1935, included the Law for the Protection of German Blood and German Honour that prohibited marriages and extramarital relations between Jews and non-Jews. A second sweeping law, the Reich Citizenship Law, stripped German Jews of their German citizenship and, since they were no longer citizens, also stripped Jews of the protection of the law. Since Jews could no longer legally claim German citizenship, it was also critical for Germany to define in law who was a German and who was a Jew. The Nuremberg Law defined a German as a person with four grandparents with "German or kindred blood." Jews were defined as anyone with three or four Jewish grandparents. A person with one or two Jewish grandparents was a *Mischling*, a crossbreed, someone of "mixed blood." Thus, who was a Jew was not determined by religious belief or tradition. It was determined by lineage. Under the law, a Jew who had converted to Christianity and his or her children and grandchildren were still legally designated as Jews. A Nazi government bureaucracy was soon busy ferreting out so-called "hidden" Jews, scouring family trees for Jewish "rot" and investigating disputed cases of Jewish designation.

The impact of the Nuremberg Laws and its Slovak facsimile, the Jewish Code, was devastating. Jews became a pariah people in the land of their birth. In Slovakia, as in Germany, interaction between Jews and non-Jews was severely restricted and violators were severely punished. The list of prohibitions went on and on and no measure designed to exclude Jews from the civil square seemed too trivial as Jewish lawyers, doctors, teachers and journalists were barred from dealing with non-Jews. Jews were denied admission to state hospitals and, after the age of fourteen, Jewish children suddenly found themselves barred from public schools.

The Slovak Jewish Code had barely been put in place when the Slovak government, a partner in Germany's war effort, also joined Nazi Germany in implementing the "Final Solution" against the Jewish population. Slovak authorities began rounding up Jews, including children, and deporting them eastward, officially to toil in labour camps but in actuality sending them to their deaths. While apologists for the Nazi puppet regime in Slovakia may argue that Slovak officials did not know that the Jews they deported were to be murdered, and for a time Slovak authorities curtailed the deportations, there is little doubt that Slovak leaders did know and willfully collaborated with the Nazis in the systematic destruction of the Slovak Jewish community. It has been estimated that approximately 70,000 Slovak Jews – almost 80 per cent of the Jewish population at the start of the war – were murdered and their property stolen by neighbours or confiscated by the Slovak state.

In the case of individual Jews whose services were deemed essential to the state economy or to community well-being, an exemption could be granted that included members of the individual's immediate family. Such an exemption was granted to Agnes's father, a respected local dentist in Bardejov. An exemption from deportation did not mean the family was exempt from oppressive provisions of the Jewish Code, however, nor did it afford any guarantee of permanent safety – an exemption could be cancelled without notice. But at least Agnes and her family avoided the deportation that proved a death sentence for the vast majority of Bardejov's almost 2,500 Jews, including many of Agnes's schoolmates. In 1942, local Bardejov authorities even prevailed upon the small group of exempt Jews to convert to Protestantism, arguing that doing so would further protect them. Again, this measure provided them with only temporary respite. As the sounds of battle crept nearer, Agnes's father learned that Bardejov was to be evacuated. Worried that his professional skills might no longer be regarded as essential enough to keep his family safe, he sent them to a small town in the interior of Slovakia, on the edge of the rugged and forested Low Tatra Mountains, where they might pass as gentiles.

As Agnes and her family sought to blend in, the tide of war was running against Germany. The 1943 Soviet victory in the Battle of Stalingrad proved a turning point in the war. With the Western allies preparing for the invasion of France, the Soviet Union went on the offensive. The Soviet Red Army pushed westward. It gradually drove German troops out of Soviet territory and, in the summer of 1944, advanced into Poland. Encouraged by the Soviets' success, anti-Nazi Slovak partisans, many operating in mountainous forested areas and joined by dissident units of the Slovak military, attempted to overthrow the collaborationist Slovak regime and link up with Soviet troops advancing from the east. The effort was crushed by the German military and Germany assumed direct charge of Slovakia.

With Germany now in control of Slovakia, the Nazis gave priority to rounding up and deporting the remaining Slovak Jews. Agnes and her family, fearing the Germans would ferret them out, escaped into the forest of the Low Tatra Mountains. Here, with other desperate Jews, they found crude shelter and foraged as best they could for food and fuel, clinging to the local anti-Nazi partisans operating in the forest for protection. As the Soviet troops finally pushed into Czechoslovakia, Agnes and her family accompanied a band of partisans on a perilous winter trek through the mountains in the hope of reaching the Soviet lines. They succeeded and, as a result, were able to count themselves among the small minority of Slovak Jews who survived the Holocaust.

Agnes was nine years old when the war began. She was fifteen when it ended with the German surrender to the Allies in the first week of May 1945. For five years Agnes and her family had avoided the deadly fate that befell the vast majority of Slovak Jews. Now, with the Holocaust finally over, Holocaust survivors faced the task of re-building their lives. It was not easy. Survivors across Europe struggled to comprehend the catastrophic destruction that had been inflicted on their communities, their families and their lives. Nowhere would life go back to the way it was. In Slovakia, many survivors – their families murdered, their property gone and their trust in their former neighbours shattered, asked themselves what they should do. Should they try to rebuild their lives in Slovakia? Should they leave? And if they left, where should they go? Who would have them? Many Slovak Holocaust survivors, hoping to begin again somewhere else, did leave and most of them collected in Jewish refugee camps in Germany and Austria. Others, perhaps undecided as to what to do or clinging to the faint hope that missing family and friends might yet return home, stayed – at least for the moment. Among those who stayed were Agnes and her immediate family.

If survivors faced an unknown future, so too did Slovakia. Recently liberated from the Nazis by the Red Army, Slovakia, with Soviet ap-proval, once again became part of a single Czechoslovak state. But pre-war ethnic tensions were quick to resurface. Anti-German sen-timent ran so high that, like many Jews, both Agnes's father and her future husband changed their family names to something "less German-sounding" – Grossmann became Gonda and Tomaschoff became Tomasov. Many Czechs who had suffered under direct Nazi rule were slow to forget that wartime Slovakia had been an indepen-dent state allied with the Nazis. And many, both Czechs and Slovaks, were not ready to forgive Britain and France for "selling them out" to the Nazis at Munich in 1938. It was the Soviet Union, not the Western allies, who had liberated Czechoslovakia from the Nazis in 1945. In free national elections in 1946, the pro-Soviet Communist Party fell short of a majority but did win the most votes and a Communist was installed as prime minister of a coalition government. Under this new government, economic reconstruction proved painfully slow and Communist popularity began to slide. Fearing that an upcoming national election would sweep them from power, the Communists seized control of the government in February 1948. The recently restored democracy evaporated as Czechoslovakia slipped into the Soviet orbit.

While the surviving Czech Jews were grateful to the Soviet Union for liberating them from the Nazis and there were individual Jews in positions of prominence both in the Communist Party and new Communist government, most Jews opposed the 1948 Communist takeover and the end of democracy. As long as Czechoslovakia's borders with the West remained open, many Jews voted with their feet. Between 1948 and 1950, almost 25,000 Jews left Czechoslovakia, most for the newly declared State of Israel. When Communist authorities closed Czechoslovakia's borders to further emigration in 1950, there were only about 18,000 Jews left in Czechoslovakia, barely 5 per cent of the pre-war Jewish population. Many of them might have left had the opportunity presented itself.

Among those Jews still in Czechoslovakia were Agnes and her family. Just eighteen when the Communists seized power, Agnes was at first less concerned with the nation's political life than with her own. While the Communist regime tightened its grip on Czechoslovakia, Agnes was preoccupied with family and friends, with school and career options, and, later, with building a life with her new husband, Joe Tomasov, who was also a Jewish survivor from Slovakia, and with raising their two children, Tomas and Katka. But there was no avoiding the scourge of antisemitism. Hollowed out of the basic freedoms we often take for granted, it was not long before Czechoslovakia turned on its remaining Jews. Antisemitism was rampant both in the Communist Party and among those who covertly despised it. Many closet anti-Communists regarded all Jews as Communists or at least Communist supporters – and, indeed, there were Jews who held senior positions in the Communist Party and government. Among them was the Party's secretary general, Rudolf Slánský. At the same time, there were also Party loyalists who mistrusted Jews, convinced that they cared more about their fellow Jews and Israel than about Czechoslovakia and the Party.

Anti-Jewish hostility spilled into the open in 1952 when, following the lead of Joseph Stalin, who initiated a purge of influential Jews in the Soviet Union, the Czechoslovak Communist Party began its own purge of Jews, including Slánský. In a notorious show trial, Slánský and thirteen other high profile Party members, eleven of them Jews, were accused of conspiring with Zionists and other non-Party elements to undermine the state. Slánský and the others were found guilty. Eleven, including Slánský, were executed. And attacks on Jews did not stop there. Many Jews were arrested and jailed. Others were simply fired from their jobs.

After the death of Stalin in January 1953, Czechoslovak leaders in Prague ordered what turned out to be but a momentary lull in their campaign of Jewish vilification. The government in Prague even approved a gradual release of "rehabilitated" Jewish prisoners. Outside Prague, however, local police and court officials were less ready to let go of antisemitism – the arrest and imprisonment of Jews continued. One of the many Czech Jews sent to prison in 1955 was Agnes's husband, Joe. He would soon have company. In 1956, Israel defeated Egypt in the Sinai War and the response from the pro-Egyptian Soviet bloc was immediate and harsh. The approximately three hundred Jews incarcerated in Czechoslovakia after the Sinai War were joined by many more Jews accused of spying for the West or engaging in Zionist activities.

The families of imprisoned Jews – as Agnes would discover when Joe was sentenced to six years in prison on trumped-up charges – found life increasingly difficult. Shunned by many of their neighbours and co-workers, and short of money, they learned that efforts to secure their loved ones' release, no matter how unjust their sentences, were seldom successful. And who might be next? No Jew felt safe in Czechoslovakia and there seemed no way out. On rare occasions, permission to leave Czechoslovakia might be granted to someone so that he or she might join family abroad, but an application for permission to leave for Israel or the West was sure to bring the authorities to the applicant's door. Much as they might want to, few Jews dared apply to leave. And any Jew caught trying to escape could count on a harsh prison sentence.

Once Joe was finally released in December 1958, Agnes Tomasov and her family focused once again on making a living, raising their children and rebuilding a home life. By the mid-1960s, restrictions in Czechoslovakia were beginning to ease and the Tomasovs were able to travel outside the Soviet bloc, to Greece and – unheard-of for Jews in the Soviet sphere – to Israel. In 1967, the situation for Jews in Czechoslovakia became precarious again, however, and, again, the flashpoint was Israel. After an escalation of tension along Israel's border with Egypt, Egypt's military closed the narrow Gulf of Aqaba to all shipping coming into and going out of Israel's southern port of Eilat. Israel declared the Egyptian blockade to be an act of war, and, when the blockade was not lifted, Israel attacked Egypt. In what soon became known as the Six-Day War, Israel defeated Egypt and its allies, who were again supported by the Soviet bloc. In retaliation for Israel's victory, Czechoslovakia joined the rest of the Soviet bloc – with the exception of Romania – in breaking off diplomatic relations with Israel. Another crackdown on Czech Jews seemed to be imminent.

But the Czechoslovak government's attention was soon focused elsewhere. After almost twenty years of Communist rule, whispered voices, among them those of the Communist Party faithful, began expressing discontent with the state repression of individual rights and free expression. Led by disgruntled intellectuals, journalists, public officials and educated professionals, there were increasing demands for greater freedom. Some dissidents even blamed Czechoslovakia's top-down decision-making process for the country's poor economic performance. But many Czechs who were agitating for change did not so much want an end to Communism as they wanted a kinder, gentler and more open Communism. Some of them also favoured decentralization and greater local autonomy, especially in Slovakia, where many people resented the political and economic influence of Prague.

Unable to still the rumblings of discontent, Czechoslovakia's hardline president, Antonín Novotný, saw his Party support erode. In the autumn of 1967, First Secretary of the regional Communist Party of Slovakia, Alexander Dubček, challenged Novotný's leadership and invited Soviet premier Leonid Brezhnev to see for himself the extent of the opposition to Novotný among the Party faithful. Brezhnev, surprised by the level of anti-Novotný sentiment, sanctioned Novotný's removal as Czechoslovakia's leader. In January 1968, Dubček replaced Novotný as First Secretary of the Czech Communist Party.

Dubček was no democrat, nor did he regard one-party rule to be problematic. The problem, as he saw it, was that the Czechoslovak Communist Party had become unresponsive to changing conditions. What was needed was a Communist Party ready to build a street-level connection with the people by demonstrating its readiness to embrace new ideas and support local and individual initiatives that promised to improve living conditions.

In April 1967, Dubček announced a far-reaching package of reforms guaranteeing, among other things, freedom of speech, freedom of the press and freedom of movement. For the first time, Joe Tomasov was able to travel to Canada to visit his sister, Aranka. There was also a pledge to reform the economy that included opening the door to entrepreneurial initiative and increasing production of quality consumer goods. Although multi-party government was not part of his reform package, Dubček promised that the expression of different and even dissenting views would be encouraged as part of the national decision-making process. As a sign that a multi-opinion if not multi-party system would be taken seriously, Dubček announced that the powers of the dreaded state security police would be cut back. He also pledged to decentralize government somewhat, by reconstituting Czechoslovakia as a federation of two equal nations – one Czech and the other Slovak. On the international level, Dubček vowed to improve relations with the West while continuing Czechoslovakia's membership in the Soviet bloc.

This reform package could not be introduced overnight and Dubček foresaw a decade-long process that would usher in "Socialism with a Human Face." Public response to Dubček's promised reforms was overwhelmingly positive and sparked a national mood of optimism referred to as the "Prague Spring." After being stifled for so long, the press was quick to test the regime's tolerance of an open and free exchange of ideas. Unthinkable only a few months earlier, newspaper articles critical of the Soviet Union and its policies began to appear. But not everyone was caught up in the spirit of reform – fearful that power was slipping through their fingers, Communist hardliners pressed Dubček to back away from his promised reforms. Instead, he raised public expectations still higher by announcing a Communist Party Congress for September 1968 that would be asked to endorse and officially implement his reform agenda.

Outside Czechoslovakia, Soviet-bloc leaders were shocked at the breadth of Dubček's reform package. They were concerned the "Prague Spring" spirit might spread and force them to introduce similar reforms. The Soviet Union pressed Dubček to accept far more limited and controlled change. Rather than court Soviet anger, Dubček pledged Czechoslovakia's continued loyalty to the Soviet-led Warsaw military pact, promised to curb "anti-socialist" tendencies, prevent the formation of rival political parties and clamp down on excesses in the press. In return, the Soviets agreed to withdraw troops it had stationed in Czechoslovakia and not interfere in Dubček's upcoming Party Congress.

To further pacify the Soviet bloc, in August 1968 a Czechoslovak delegation joined those from the Soviet Union, East Germany, Poland, Hungary and Bulgaria in signing the Bratislava Declaration that affirmed support for Marxism-Leninism and opposed all "anti-socialist" forces. After the Bratislava conference, Soviet troops withdrew from Czechoslovakia but remained strategically deployed along the Czech border.

The Bratislava Declaration aside, the Soviet Union saw no on-the-ground change to Dubček's plans and grew increasingly convinced that his pledges of loyalty to the Soviet bloc were just empty words. Before the fever for reform could spread beyond Czechoslovak borders, Soviet-bloc leaders agreed to put an end to the whole business once and for all. On the night of August 20, 1968, twenty thousand Soviet-bloc troops backed by two thousand tanks from the Soviet Union, Bulgaria, Poland and Hungary invaded Czechoslovakia. That very day, Joe Tomasov had been sent to an international conference in Sweden. In the ensuing turmoil, he was stranded outside the country for two weeks. Recalling the bloodshed of the Hungarian uprising in 1956, Dubček called on the Czechoslovak population not to resist the invaders and Czechoslovak troops were ordered to remain in their barracks. In spite of widespread public outrage at the invasion, incidents of scattered resistance and even reported instances of individuals pleading with the advancing troops to turn around and go home, the Prague Spring was finished. Gustav Husak, once a reformer sympathetic to Dubček, was installed as head of the Czech Communist Party. A purge of reformers followed.

Many Czechs and Slovaks did not wait to see how post-Dubček Czechoslovakia would fare. In the confusion following the Soviet-bloc invasion, Czechoslovakia's borders with Germany and Austria lay open. Seizing the moment, 70,000 Czech citizens fled westward – among them were an estimated 3,400 Czechoslovakian Jews, including Agnes, her husband and their children.

Most of these refugees eventually settled abroad. Agnes and her family were selected to come to Canada as part of a Canadian government refugee resettlement scheme. Few among these Czechoslovak refugees likely knew that the path they followed to Canada had been paved by others. First among them were Displaced Persons. At the end of World War II, Europe was awash in refugees, commonly referred to as Displaced Persons or simply DPs. Canada at first rejected any notion that it might offer sanctuary to any of these DPs. Restrictionist Canadian immigration regulations in place at the end of the war severely limited immigration of southern and eastern Europeans in general and Jews in particular. Nor was there any significant pressure on the Canadian government to change the regulations – there was certainly no great public outcry demanding that Canada's door be opened to the hundreds of thousands of DPs languishing in refugee camps in Germany, Austria and Italy. With regard to these refugees, Canada initially supported a plan to repatriate all of them back to their countries of original citizenship. The government reasoned that if refugees went home, there wouldn't be any refugee problem. When it became clear that more than a million DPs would not voluntarily agree to repatriation – particularly Holocaust survivors who were forever uprooted from their former homes and non-Jewish DPs who refused to return to homelands that were now within the Soviet orbit – Canada denied it had any obligation, moral or otherwise, to take them in.

How is it then that thousands of DPs eventually resettled in Canada? It was certainly not out of humanitarian concern for the refugees. Canada's eventual interest in taking in thousands of DPs was out of self-interest: In 1945, many economists predicted that, without the economic engine of wartime spending, Canada and the West more generally was poised to slip back into a 1930s-like depression. They were wrong – after a lumbering start, the post-war Canadian economy expanded rapidly. The demand for Canadian goods and services grew both at home and abroad. For the first time since the 1929 onset of the Great Depression, the biggest peacetime economic problem was not unemployment but a shortage of workers to meet the nation's job needs.

By late 1946, labour-intensive Canadian industries were lobbying Ottawa to relax immigration restrictions to permit the import of immigrant labour. Big business may have been bullish on immigration; the Canadian public, however, remained skeptical. Would the economic recovery continue? Those whose memories were shaped in the hungry 1930s harboured doubts. Furthermore, Canadian immigration officials, who for many years saw their duty as guarding the Canadian gate against all newcomers, were also unsympathetic to renewed immigration if it meant the influx of DPs – and especially of the Jewish DPs who stood first in Europe's exit line. The public seemed to agree with them. A 1946 public opinion poll found that Canadians would rather see recently defeated Germans allowed into Canada than Jews.

But anti-immigration forces would be outflanked. Bolstered by optimistic projections for continuing Canadian economic growth, in 1947 the government announced it would re-open Canada's door to immigration, nevertheless holding fast to ethnic and racial selectivity. Thus, priority was given to recruiting immigrants assumed to have a proven ability to assimilate – settlers from the United Kingdom, Western Europe and the United States. Accordingly, immigration recruitment in Britain and Western Europe, particularly Holland, was the first to get underway.

Labour-intensive industries, pleased by the government's re-opening of immigration, were less pleased with the rules on ethnic selectivity, arguing that, for the economic boom to continue, employers needed access to the DP labour pool. The government grudgingly agreed, even as it continued to monitor the public mood for any negative reaction to the arrival of DPs – and especially to the arrival of Jews. When negative public response turned out to be far less than the government feared and the demand for labour continued to grow, racially and ethnically based immigration restrictions against eastern and southern Europeans, including Holocaust survivors, were gradually lifted.

In 1956, when the DP labour pool had dried up, the Hungarian refugee crisis erupted. That year, a popularly supported uprising against Communist rule in Hungary was crushed by invading Soviet-bloc troops. As the last flickers of anti-Communist resistance were being extinguished, a flood of Hungarian refugees poured westward into neighbouring Austria, just as the wave of escaped Czechoslovakians would arrive twelve years later. The plight of exiled refugee Hungarian "freedom fighters" touched Canadians. The public and press called on the Canadian government to act with generosity in offering Hungarian refugees a Canadian home. But Ottawa remained cautious. Federal security personnel quietly warned that the Soviet bloc was using this refugee crisis to plant spies in unsuspecting Western countries, including Canada. The Canadian government, for its part, seemed less concerned with spies than with who would pay the cost of a Hungarian resettlement program.

As the government dithered, public pressure on them to take action continued to build. Private agencies and provincial governments stepped forward with pledges of financial support for refugee resettlement. Press from all sides of the political spectrum castigated the government for its inaction in the face of human suffering. Hard pressed, the government finally announced that a path had been cut through the jungle of immigration red tape. The minister of immigration hurried off to Vienna and hard on his heels came immigration teams assigned to skim off the cream of the Hungarian refugees before other refugee-receiving countries got them first. Routine immigration procedures, including medical and security checks, were set aside until after the refugees arrived in Canada. In relatively short order, almost 37,000 Hungarians were resettled in Canada.

In spite of the success of this refugee resettlement program, immigration officials insisted the Hungarian episode was a one-time exception to normal immigration procedures. Time would prove them wrong. In 1968, as the Prague Spring was being crushed by Soviet-bloc tanks, thousands of Czech and Slovak refugees, including Agnes and Joe Tomasov and their two children, crossed out of Czechoslovakia into the West. It was a replay of the Hungarian episode as the Canadian public and media demanded the Canadian government act quickly and with compassion in bringing its fair share of Czechoslovak refugees into Canada. This time, without stalling, the Canadian government approved a program to bring thousands of homeless but well-educated Czech and Slovak refugees to Canada. Between September 1968 and the end of 1969, Canada took in approximately 12,000 Czech and Slovak refugees. And Canada did well by doing so. These refugees were disproportionately young, well-educated and skilled. About 70 per cent of refugee household heads were in their child-rearing years and many – including Agnes and Joe Tomasov, an engineer – were skilled professionals with post-secondary education. The Tomasovs resettled in Toronto and built successful new lives for themselves, for their children – now called Tom and Kathy – and for their grandchildren.

There is an expression in Yiddish that roughly translates as "People plan and God laughs." Whatever her parents might have planned for Agnes when she was born, no one – not her parents, not Agnes, not anyone else – could have imagined how the twists and turns of history would shape Agnes's life. But Agnes has proved herself no victim of history. As a child survivor of the Holocaust, as a young wife and mother in anti-Jewish post-war Communist Czechoslovakia, as an accidental immigrant to Canada, Agnes has refused to concede her independence of mind or action. To the contrary, she has pushed back against the very idea of defeat. Her determination to openly and honestly share her story with others is very much in character.

Harold Troper
University of Toronto | OISE
2010

SOURCES AND SUGGESTIONS FOR FURTHER READING:

Case, Holly. "Territorial revision and the Holocaust: Hungary and Slovakia during World War II." In Doris L. Bergen, *Lessons and Legacies VIII: From Generation to Generation*. Evanston, IL: Northwestern University Press, 2008, 222–246.

Cornwall, Mark. *Czechoslovakia in a Nationalist and Fascist Europe, 1918–1948*. New York: Oxford University Press, 2007.

Dagan, Avigdor. *Jews of Czechoslovakia: Historical Studies and Surveys*, Vol. 3. Philadelphia: Jewish Publication Society of America, 1984.

Dirks, Gerald E. *Canada's Refugee Policy: Indifference or Opportunism?* Montreal: McGill-Queen's University Press, 1977.

Fatran, Gila. "Slovakia: Historical introduction." In *The Encyclopedia of the Righteous Among the Nations: Rescuers of Jews during the Holocaust, Vol. I*, ed. Israel Gutman. Jerusalem: Yad Vashem, 2003.

Kamenec, Ivan. *On the Trail of Tragedy: The Holocaust in Slovakia*. Bratislava: H & H Publishing, 2007.

Kelley, Ninette, and Michael J. Trebilcock. *The Making of the Mosaic: A History of Canadian Immigration Policy*. Toronto: University of Toronto Press, 1998.

Rothkirchen, Livia. *The Jews of Bohemia and Moravia: Facing the Holocaust*. Lincoln, NE: University of Nebraska Press, 2005.

Willams, Kieran. *The Prague Spring and Its Aftermath: Czechoslovak Politics, 1968–1970*. New York: Cambridge University Press, 1997.

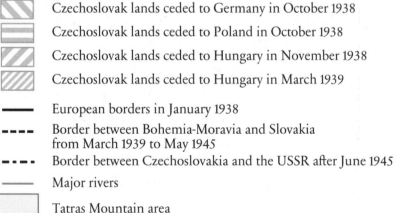

Czechoslovak lands ceded to Germany in October 1938

Czechoslovak lands ceded to Poland in October 1938

Czechoslovak lands ceded to Hungary in November 1938

Czechoslovak lands ceded to Hungary in March 1939

European borders in January 1938

Border between Bohemia-Moravia and Slovakia
from March 1939 to May 1945

Border between Czechoslovakia and the USSR after June 1945

Major rivers

Tatras Mountain area

© 2010 - The Azrieli Foundation

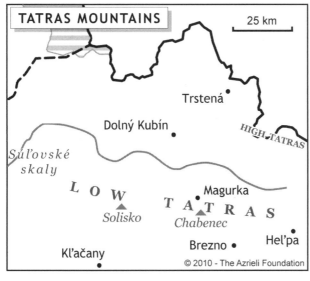

TATRAS MOUNTAINS

25 km

© 2010 - The Azrieli Foundation

Historical and Geographical Timeline: Czechoslovakia 1918-1968

Czechoslovakia's borders shifted several times over the course of the period covered in Agnes Tomasov's memoir, and often in ways that had a direct impact on the course of her story. The map on the previous pages depicts both the border changes and the towns and cities that are mentioned in her memoir and the following is a timeline of these changes.

1918 Following the end of World War I, the Republic of Czechoslovakia is created at the Paris Peace Conference. It is made up of the states of Slovakia, Moravia, Austrian Silesia, Bohemia and Carpathian Ruthenia that were formerly part of the Austro-Hungarian Empire. Tomáš Masaryk is elected first president of the newly independent state.

1920 Czechoslovakia's new constitution establishes a centralized parliamentary system and, over the course of the 1920s and 1930s, the country enjoys relative political stability.

1933 Hitler comes to power in Germany.

1935 Tomáš Masaryk steps down as president and is replaced by foreign minister Edvard Beneš.

September 1935 The Nazis introduce the Nuremberg Laws that strip Jews of their civil rights as German citizens and separate them from Germans legally, socially and politically.

November 9–10, 1938 A series of planned attacks against Jews over the course of twenty-four hours, Kristallnacht – the "Night of Broken Glass" – is often seen as an important turning point in Hitler's policies of systematic persecution of Jews.

May-September 1938 Hitler demands that the Sudetenland, a Czech border area principally comprised of ethnic Germans, be ceded to Germany. On September 30, Germany, Britain and France sign an agreement in Munich that allows the Sudeten territory to be incorporated into the German empire.

October 2, 1938 Poland is awarded the area of Těšín, an important coal mining centre in which 35 per cent of the population are Poles.

November 2, 1938 Hungary gains over one million hectares of Czechoslovakian territory along their border in the so-called Vienna Award. Levice, the birthplace of Agnes Tomasov's mother and the home of her maternal grandparents, uncle and cousins becomes part of Hungary, as does Košice, the town where Agnes's mother died. Bardejov, where Agnes Tomasov lives with her family, remains part of what is now called the Czecho-Slovak Republic.

March 15, 1939 Hitler breaks the Munich Agreement and invades and occupies the Czech territories of Bohemia and Moravia, establishing them as a German protectorate. Although the Slovak Republic is granted nominal independence under the right-wing regime of the Catholic Hlinka (Slovak) Peoples' Party led by Father Jozef Tiso, it is controlled by and allied with Nazi Germany. Nonetheless, the areas of Slovakia where Agnes Tomasov lives do not come under direct German occupation until October 1944. By the end of March 1939, the independent Republic of Czechoslovakia has completely ceased to exist.

April 18, 1939 Slovakia begins passing its own version of the Nuremberg Laws. Later that month, Jews are dismissed from government positions.

September 1, 1939 Germany invades Poland and World War II begins.

September 19, 1939 Slovak Jews are expelled from the military. Many more discriminatory laws follow. Jewish children are expelled from schools, for example, and Jews are barred from public recreational facilities. Between 1940 and 1941, Jews lose most of their civil rights.

April-November 1940 New anti-Jewish laws escalate discrimination and marginalization of Jews in Slovakia. The First Aryanization Act, for example, requires the transfer of Jewish-owned property to non-Jews; Jews are required to register with the government and state their financial status; and the Second Aryanization Act completes the transfer and liquidation of any businesses still owned by Jews. By the end of this period, Jews have been almost completely excluded from social and economic life.

June 22, 1941 Germany invades the USSR and compels Slovakia to join the invasion forces. Although successful at the beginning, the German invasion soon bogs down.

September 9, 1941 Slovakia passes the "Jewish Code," which contains an additional 270 anti-Jewish measures, including a measure ordering Jews to wear a yellow Star of David.

April 18, 1942 About 400 Slovakian Jews are deported to Auschwitz.

May–October 1942 More than 2,000 Jews from Bardejov, where Agnes Tomasov lives, are deported to the Lublin district in Poland. By the end of this period, more than 58,000 Jews have been deported from Slovakia to Poland, where most are murdered in Sobibor or Auschwitz.

November 1942 The Battle of Stalingrad begins.

February 1943 German forces surrender to the Soviet army at Stalingrad – a key military turning point in the war. From that point on, Germany is never able to regain the offensive in the east. Throughout the rest of 1943, Soviet offensives liberate most of Russia, Belorussia and the Ukraine.

March 1944 Groups of anti-Nazi Slovaks begin a plan to overthrow the collaborationist Slovak government and their Nazi protectors and link up with Soviet forces in the mountainous border area between Poland and Slovakia.

June 1944 More than 1,000 Jews are deported to Auschwitz from Levice, where Agnes's grandmother lives.

Summer 1944 The Soviet Red Army advances into eastern Poland.

August 27, 1944 Soviet partisans kill twenty-eight Germans in central Slovakia; Germany announces the occupation of Slovakia two days later, and the anti-government and anti-Nazi uprising, known as the Slovak National Uprising, begins.

August 31, 1944 The anti-government and anti-Nazi partisans are defeated in eastern and western Slovakia by the Germans.

September 1944 The turning point in the war for central Slovakia, where Agnes and her family are hiding out in the Low Tatra Mountains. Fierce fighting continues between Soviet and German forces on Slovakian soil in the months that follow, with different areas changing hands at various times. At one pivotal point, Agnes and her family are surrounded by German forces and decide on a fateful course of action.

October 28, 1944 The Slovak National Uprising is officially quelled by the Germans.

Late 1944 and early 1945 The territories of pre-war Czechoslovakia are liberated by the Soviet Red Army with some help from Czech and Slovak resistance.

May 1945 Soviet troops liberate Prague and occupy most of pre-1938 Czechoslovakia.

May 9, 1945 Germany surrenders to Soviet forces in Berlin, ending the war in Europe.

May 16, 1945 With Soviet approval, Edvard Beneš and his government-in-exile return to Prague to re-establish a liberal democratic regime in a newly restored Czechoslovakian republic. With the exception of Subcarpathian Ruthenia, which is annexed by the Soviet Union, Czechoslovakia returns to its pre-war borders.

September 1945 Japan surrenders to Allied forces and World War II officially ends.

October 28, 1945 The National Assembly unanimously confirms Beneš as president of the Czech republic.

May 26, 1946 In the first post-war democratic election, the Communist Party of Czechoslovakia emerges as the single largest group, with 38 per cent of the vote. Klement Gottwald, leader of the Communist Party, is named prime minister in a coalition cabinet with socialists and Beneš's liberal followers.

February 1948 The Communist Party and trade unions stage a bloodless coup d'état that ends democracy in Czechoslovakia for more than forty years. The Communist Party of Czechoslovakia is brought under direct Soviet control in a series of Communist Party purges that follow the model of those in the USSR.

1949–1955 Israel is considered to be an enemy of Communism, and anti-Jewish sentiment in the Communist Party of Czechoslovakia increases radically. Any perceived tie to Israel and Zionism is harshly punished and many local, high-ranking and old-line Jewish communists are replaced by leaders devoted to the Soviet regime; some are executed after being convicted of treason and espionage at show trials.

1948–1968 Life in Czechoslovakia is largely geared to the economic needs of Soviet reconstruction – capitalist enterprises are no longer allowed, agriculture is forcibly collectivized and former trade patterns with the West are broken. Forced contributions to Soviet reconstruction delay Eastern European economic recovery and make life difficult for ordinary people. Life is permeated by the ideology of Soviet-style communism, though sometimes with a high degree of cynicism. It becomes impossible to travel to non-Soviet bloc countries and people live in fear of being denounced to the security police – a fear that becomes all too real for Agnes and her family.

1953 Joseph Stalin and Czech Communist leader Klement Gottwald die.

January 5, 1968 Alexander Dubček replaces Antonín Novotný as First Secretary of the Communist Party of Czechoslovakia, ushering in the period of reform known as the Prague Spring.

August 20, 1968 Soviet-led Warsaw Pact troops invade Czechoslovakia, putting an end to the Prague Spring.

To my beloved children, grandchildren
and great-grandchildren

Ledor Vador…

Agnes Tomasov's Family Tree*

GRANDPARENTS (father's parents):
Hermann and Katherine Grossmann

FATHER:
Edmund Grossmann (later Gonda)

UNCLE (father's brother):
Sanyi

Married: *Jolan*

STEPMOTHER:
Children: *Evike and Katka*   *Sarolta Neuman*

UNCLE (father's brother):   STEP-AUNT:
Joska   *Elisabeth*

Married: Margit

STEP-AUNT:
Children: *Heda and Pista*   *Irene*

STEP-UNCLE:
AUNT (father's sister):   *Miklos*
Aranka

BROTHER:
Ivan
born 1934

Married:
Hedika Bergmann

NIECE:
Ivetka

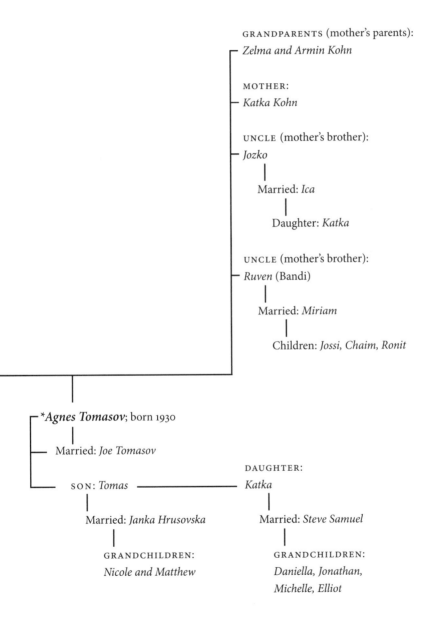

GRANDPARENTS (mother's parents):
Zelma and Armin Kohn

MOTHER:
Katka Kohn

UNCLE (mother's brother):
Jozko

Married: *Ica*

Daughter: *Katka*

UNCLE (mother's brother):
Ruven (Bandi)

Married: *Miriam*

Children: *Jossi, Chaim, Ronit*

*Agnes Tomasov; born 1930

Married: *Joe Tomasov*

SON: *Tomas* ———————

Married: *Janka Hrusovska*

GRANDCHILDREN:
Nicole and Matthew

DAUGHTER:
Katka

Married: *Steve Samuel*

GRANDCHILDREN:
Daniella, Jonathan, Michelle, Elliot

Prologue

I was only twenty-one months old when my dear mother died. I was born in the small, primarily Jewish town of Bardejov in northeastern Slovakia – then part of Czechoslovakia – on June 16, 1930, and my mother left me on March 17, 1932. In spirit, however, I believe that she never abandoned me. In this memoir, I never write the words "late mother" because, even at the advanced age of seventy-three, I feel that my mother is always with me.

My mother, Katka Grossmann, née Katka Kohn, was born on March 20, 1907, in Levice, Czechoslovakia and died in Košice, Czechoslovakia, before she had reached the age of twenty-five.[1] Aside from being beautiful, she was also intelligent and educated – she worked as a legal secretary in a lawyer's office. She supported her parents, Zelma and Armin Kohn, as well as one of her brothers, Jozko, who attended university in Prague, the capital and cultural centre of Czechoslovakia. Her other brother Ruven, whom we called Bandi, was a member of the Zionist youth movement Hashomer Hatzair.[2]

---

1 Levice is in western Slovakia, about twenty-five kilometres from the Hungarian border. In 1930, it had a population of just over 8,000, of whom about 1,400 were Jewish. Košice, about 265 kilometres east of Levice, was a city of 70,000 in 1930 with a Jewish population of 11,000.

2 Meaning in Hebrew "the Young Guard," Hashomer Hatzair was a left-wing Zion-

Until I was seven years old, I had no idea that I had lost my mother, but I remember looking forward to staying at my grandparents' house in Levice every summer. I remember how loved I felt there – I was the centre of attention and adored my grandparents. In 1937, though, on the first day of school, something happened that changed my world forever. My Grade 2 teacher, Ondrušková, welcomed us and asked how we had spent our summer vacation. I was the first to report my travel experiences: I had spent most of my summer vacation in Levice, where I was the princess of the family. For the last few days of my vacation, my uncle Jozko had taken me to Lučenec to visit my other grandparents (my father's parents). And, from there, we stopped over in Prešov, the place of my third set of grandparents (at that time, I didn't know that they were my stepmother's parents). I reported to my classmates that during the summer I had visited all three sets of my grandparents. They burst out laughing. Nobody had three sets of grandparents, they said. I insisted that I wasn't lying, that I really had three sets of grandparents. The teacher pulled me aside and tried to calm me down. She told me that she knew that I was telling the truth, but that the children were also right: "You, as a clever girl, should know that if you have two parents, you can have only two sets of grandparents. In your case it is different, because your birth mother passed away."

I remember it as though it happened yesterday. I started to cry and ran away, far from the classroom. I arrived home, breathless, and ran into the kitchen shouting, "Thank God, Mommy, you are alive. My teacher told me that you had died!" I explained to her what had happened at school. I hugged her, overjoyed that she was alive, still not understanding the sad truth. She took me into the living room

---

ist youth organization that was particularly active in east-central Europe before and immediately after World War II. For more information, see the glossary.

and locked the door behind us. My stepmother didn't have many maternal qualities, but she was intelligent. She told me that what the teacher had said was true, and that what she was about to tell me now had to remain a secret between the two of us until I got married. If my father found out what she was about to disclose, she would be forced to leave with my younger brother, Ivanko – my half-brother. These words became engraved in my soul as one of the deepest, most painful experiences of my young life. "Your birth mother really died," she said. "God sent me to replace her on this earth." She asked me once more to keep this a secret and to not reveal it to anybody, not even to my maternal grandparents in Levice.

Hearing all this was a deep shock, and, since I had sworn not to tell anybody, I had to cope with it all by myself. I thought it may have been my fault that my mother died, that I caused it to happen, and I went through terrible emotional distress. But I kept my promise and never told anybody my secret. I didn't even tell my maternal grandmother, although I felt much closer to her after I found out the awful truth. In the first place, I didn't want to break my promise to my stepmother and, secondly, in my naïve mind, I thought that perhaps my grandmother didn't know that her daughter had died. I didn't want to cause her the same pain that I had just gone through. But I started to notice things that I hadn't paid attention to before. For example, on the night table beside my grandmother's bed was a photo of a beautiful young lady. Every evening, before going to bed, we both would kiss the photo; sometimes we also picked flowers and placed them beside the picture. My grandmother had told me that it was a photo of her youngest sister, Katka. Now, for the first time, I was almost sure that it was my mother. From that moment on, if no one was around, I would not only kiss the photo, but also whisper to her how deeply I missed her.

There were still times, though, that, in the depth of my heart, I didn't want to admit that I didn't have a mother, so I convinced myself that maybe I had misunderstood what I had been told. My mother might come back, I thought; I just had to be patient. So, twice a day, I would go to the railway station to wait for her. When somebody close to the age of my mother got out of the train, I would follow her, hoping that she might recognize me. I did this for a long, long time. Each night I would fall asleep, hoping that the next day I would have better luck and we would find each other.

Family and Childhood

My parents met in Levice in 1926. My mother, Katka Kohn, was nineteen and my father, Edmund Grossmann, was twenty-five. My father had come from the small Jewish community of Lučenec, in the south-central Slovakian region of Czechoslovakia, to Levice, a town over eighty kilometres away, to get some practical experience as a dentist before his upcoming examinations. I don't know the exact date of their wedding, although it must have been sometime between 1926 and 1929.

In response to an advertisement for a dentist's position, they left together for Bardejov, where they found themselves in a world that was completely different from the one they had come from. Out of a population of five thousand, about three thousand were poor, ultra-Orthodox Jews. At first, the Hasidic Jews shunned them, but the young, good-looking couple was, after some time, accepted by them, as well as by the rest of the Jewish community.[1]

---

1 Orthodox Judaism encompasses a set of beliefs and practices characterized by strict religious observance of Jewish dietary laws, restrictions on work on the Sabbath and holidays, and a modest code of dress. The Hasidic movement, a branch of ultra-Orthodox Judaism, was founded in the eighteenth century by Rabbi Israel ben Eliezer and is based on the philosophy of joyful prayer, spirituality and mysticism. For more information, see the glossary.

My uncle Jozko travelled the two hundred kilometres from Levice to visit his sister every week. On March 17, 1932, he arrived in Bardejov for his regular visit to find my father waiting for him at the railway station, to tell Uncle Jozko that his beloved sister Katka had passed away that morning at the hospital in Košice. Jozko collapsed from the news, and had to be taken to the hospital by ambulance. Later that day, the whole family travelled from Levice to Košice. My grandparents had lost their only daughter, and my uncles Jozko and Ruven, their only sister. It was a tragedy for the whole family. My mother had a large extended family in Levice – her mother had five married sisters with children – and they were all very close.

As I've said, I was just a baby at the time and was unaware of what was going on while I was playing in Bardejov with my nanny, whom I called "Mamma." My grandmother had also been staying with me in Bardejov for awhile, but following my mother's death she began to have heart problems. My grandfather's health started to deteriorate as well. My grandparents apparently moved around a lot – I later found out that my relatives supported my grandfather by buying him one business after another, but he really didn't have any business sense. He went bankrupt every time.

In 1933, when I wasn't quite three years old, my father re-married. My new stepmother, Sarolta Neuman, was from nearby Prešov; she had two sisters, Elisabeth and Irene, and a brother, Miklos.

My brother, Ivan, was born in Bardejov on August 17, 1934, when I was four years old. I was staying with my grandparents in Levice and plans were made for my uncle Jozko to take me to Bardejov to see my new little brother. The whole family gathered in my grandparents' modest apartment to say goodbye and accompany me to the railway station. Uncle Jozko held a high position in the railway service. He wore an elegant uniform and I was very proud of him as he carried me in his arms through the town.

Uncle Jozko and I travelled in the first-class compartment. The windows were open and Jozko pointed to flying storks in the sky, telling me that they had brought me my brother. All the way to Bardejov I stood at the window and thanked all the storks for the gift of my baby brother. After travelling for seven hours, we arrived in Bardejov, where my family showed me a big, black baby carriage with little Ivan in it. I loved him from that first moment and was so protective of him that whenever he cried, I demanded that he be fed immediately.

My maternal grandfather died in 1937. I don't know very much about his death and I have only a few recollections of him. I remember having a "black market" agreement with him that my grandmother didn't know about. We would exchange ice cream for bread with goose fat. I wasn't allowed to eat ice cream because I had chronic tonsillitis and, at that time, people thought that eating cold food actually caused tonsillitis to flare up; my grandfather wasn't allowed to eat bread with goose fat because he was a diabetic and wasn't supposed to eat high-fat foods. He would ask me to get slices of bread from my grandmother, who was pleased that I seemed to have such a good appetite. I would take it straight to my grandfather, who in turn bought me ice cream.

The last apartment in Levice where my grandmother lived with her sons after my grandfather's death was Schollerova 24. It was a long, one-storey house divided into three separate apartments with one shared bathroom. My grandmother's apartment was in the middle; I slept with her in the first bedroom and my uncles slept in the rear bedroom. The kitchen was in the front. It was a rather poor accommodation, but I loved it at the time.

Not all of my relatives on my mother's side lived so modestly. My great-aunt, Linka Knapp, was married to her first cousin, a bank manager at Tekovska Banka, and they were very rich. This position was quite rare among Jews and they were at the top of Levice society. To me, Linka was like a countess – they had a gorgeous house with servants. Their only son, Paul, was born with one eye – most likely because his parents were first cousins; on the advice of their doctor, they didn't have any more children.

~

In 1938, the political situation in Europe began to change drastically, but, at the age of eight, I wasn't yet aware of it. I do remember my father listening to the British Broadcasting Corporation (BBC) – German radio spread only propaganda to incite the hatred and persecution of Jews.

The summer of 1938 was the last I would spend with my grandmother and the rest of my mother's family in Levice, and it remains in my memory to this day. Two events in particular stand out for me. The first is the arrival of a theatre group from Budapest. My grandmother took me to see them and I remember sitting in her lap as we watched the show. The play, called *János Vitéz* (Sir John), was about a young girl, Iluska, who drowned in the lake, and her lover, who pleaded with the lake to return his beloved. My grandmother cried bitterly; I knew she was thinking of her daughter. I cried too, but still didn't break the promise I had made to my stepmother.

The second notable event for me was seeing the entire Jewish community gathered at the railway station to say goodbye to a group of boys and girls leaving for Palestine. The young people all belonged to the Zionist movement Hashomer Hatzair and had gone through training for settlement in Palestine in Svati Benedikt, close to Levice. Among them was Uncle Ruven, my mother's youngest brother. I went to the train station with my grandmother and all our relatives. They carried me on their shoulders and we all danced the hora, a traditional Jewish dance of celebration, but there were also lots of tears. It was hard for the parents to see their children leave, but I admire and respect their foresight in letting them go – I know now that it saved them from certain death. At the time, though, I tried to cheer up my grandmother by saying, "Don't cry, Babi, Bandi is not so good-looking – you still have a more handsome son, Jozko." Uncle Jozko joked about my remark for many years after.

In August 1938, just before I left to return to Bardejov, the whole family got together as usual to say goodbye. They all came to the railway station to see me off and we all seemed to share the same sense of foreboding that this would be my last visit. I was heartbroken at the thought of never returning to the place where I felt so loved.

As it turned out, we were right – these are my last childhood memories from Levice. I didn't have a chance to visit Levice again the next summer because in March 1939, Levice and Lučenec were both occupied by Hungary, while Bardejov remained part of Slovakia. Everything changed.

I came home to my family in Bardejov, but I felt like an orphan. Nonetheless, I still went to school. I played. I laughed. I joked around like the other children. I had a girlfriend in Bardejov named Magda Neumann. We had been best friends ever since nursery school, when she took me home after I peed in my pants. It was always nice to see her after being away all summer.

When I returned to Bardejov I found a belated surprise birthday present that my father ordered from out of the country. It was a doll that was considered miraculous at the time because she could open and close her eyes when she was tilted. I was so excited that I took the doll to bed with me and couldn't sleep all night. The next day I took her to school, where all the girls admired her.

On the way home, I walked through the park and a huge crowd of girls followed me, even girls older than me. All of a sudden one of the older girls grabbed the doll away from me and exclaimed, "Can't you see that your doll is dead? We have to arrange a funeral and bury her immediately!" The girls had chosen a burial place next to the fence at the park. They dug a hole and performed a burial ceremony, placing my doll in the ground. I cried inconsolably and they sent me home. When I explained the tragedy to my father, he was furious. He screamed at me, grabbed my hand and demanded that I show him where the doll was buried. We arrived at the burial spot less than half an hour after the "funeral," but not a single girl was there. My beautiful doll had disappeared from her grave.

My father was extremely angry with me and told me how stupid I was – even after the "funeral," I firmly believed that my doll had really died. My father punished me by vowing to never again buy me another doll and he kept his word. Afterward, I tried to make myself a makeshift doll out of rags. I think my own mother would have forgiven my naïveté and would have bought me a simple doll to replace the one that I had lost– this was a time that I really missed her.

That fall, my father was drafted into the army as a result of a general mobilization to defend Czechoslovakia. He was assigned to Komárno, a town on the Danube that bordered Hungary. My stepmother, Ivanko (as we called my little brother) and I left for Prešov to be with my stepmother's mother and her sisters. Her youngest sister, Irene, was married to a photographer. Both Irene and her sister Elisabeth were always nice to me and I have fond memories of them, but my stepmother and stepgrandmother devoted all their attention to Ivan, and I was just barely tolerated. At night, I would cry for my grandmother and the rest of my relatives in Levice, and also for my father. I prayed to my dear mother to watch over my father.

My stepmother hired a young girl to take care of me and Ivanko in Prešov. She would take us to the closest park – the Gardista zahrada (Garden of the Guard), which had been recently renamed in honour of the Hlinka Guard. This was the paramilitary unit of Hlinka's Slovak People's Party that had since November 1938 led a government allied with Nazi Germany.[2] It was the Hlinka Guard that would later be responsible for the rounding up and deportation of Slovak Jews to forced labour and death camps. I don't remember exactly how long we were in Prešov, but for me it was too long.

---

2   In March 1939, Slovakia was granted independence from Czechoslovakia after signing a treaty with Germany that made them a German Protectorate and political ally. Closely allied with Germany until 1944, Slovakia was not occupied by the Germans until October 1944. Slovakia was ruled by the nationalist, totalitarian Slovak People's Party that established their own antisemitic laws modelled on the Nazis.

~

Looking back, I can see how much my childhood was marked with anticipation of the war and the war itself – fortunately, perhaps, I didn't understand then how much I was affected by it. I was only nine years old when tragedy struck Slovakia and not yet fifteen when World War II ended.

On April 18, 1939, just over a month after the new Slovak state was officially proclaimed, its collaborationist government legislated its first anti-Jewish law: "a definition of the Jews," which classified Jews by religion. Other new laws soon followed, such as the "aryanization" of Jewish-owned businesses ("legally" transferring their property to non-Jewish citizens) and confiscation of their valuables, such as furs and jewellery. The government banned intermarriages and restricted Jews from certain modes of travel, no longer allowing them to drive cars or travel in first and second-class trains.

In 1939, Jews and gentiles were still in public schools together and most of the non-Jewish children treated us horribly. We couldn't play in the park in the middle of the town: a sign at the entrance read, "JEWS AND DOGS ARE NOT ALLOWED HERE." I would look enviously at the gentile children who were playing there and think, "Why can't I be like them?"

We were restricted from all forms of entertainment. We were taken from school directly to our houses and I could only play inside with a few of my friends, Magda Neumann, Sipos and my non-Jewish friends, Eva Korinkova and Anna Simkova. But, as children will do, we still tried to have a little fun and one day my friend Magda suggested we go to a football game. This was strictly prohibited for Jews, but we went anyway. Unfortunately Mrs. Grofcik, whose husband was a high-ranking police officer, noticed us and began shrieking, "Jewish children are here; Jewish children are here!" We started to run. I felt a policeman grab me. He happened to be a patient of my father's, so he took me home and told my father what happened, asking him to punish me, which he did. I was not permitted to meet my friends anymore. I was devastated.

Public school was a daily grim experience until, in 1941, when I was eleven, the authorities threw us out of the public school and forced us to attend a separate Jewish school. Despite the shock of having to leave our school, we were happier than we had been in the regular public school where we had suffered so much humiliation.

The next step in the process of our degradation happened in the fall of 1941 with the establishment of forced labour camps in Sered, Nováky and Vyhne. On March 9, 1942, the Jewish star, which had become compulsory to wear on the outside of our clothes on September 9, 1941, was enlarged from two and a half inches to four inches. As a child who didn't understand the implications, I was actually proud to wear this yellow Jewish star.

On April 18, 1942, hundreds of horse-drawn carriages arrived from neighbouring villages bringing Jewish families to Bardejov; they were driven to the train station – at that time we didn't know where they were being taken.[3] Almost one month later, on May 15, 1942, all of Bardejov's Jews were rounded up in the main synagogue and smaller houses of worship. My father was allowed an exemption by the minister of the interior because, as a dentist, he was considered to be providing an essential service. The deportation of the Jews who were being detained in the synagogues began on May 15, 1942; we found out much later that they had been deported to the Lublin district in Poland. They were crushed into cattle wagons, eighty people in each, without any food or water. The deportations continued in Bardejov until October 1942. By then, in total, over 58,000 Jews had been deported from Slovakia to Poland, over 2,000 of them from my hometown of Bardejov.[4]

---

3   The Jews who were rounded up in Bardejov were deported to Auschwitz, the site of a complex of concentration camps that included the Birkenau death camp. For more information on Auschwitz, see the glossary.

4   Most of the Jews deported from Slovakia to Poland were murdered in the Sobibor and Auschwitz death camps.

Altogether only seven Jewish families, including our own, were spared because they were designated as essential to the economy. According to the new laws, my father's exemption could cover his immediate family and two close relatives, so my stepmother's mother and her brother, Miklos, moved into our house. Our Jewish school was closed in 1942; the remaining few of us were placed back into the public school system. It was a miserable situation for us – the gentile students and teachers had only contempt for us. One of my Jewish friends, Vera Grosswirth, was in my class – her parents were also exempt because they were doctors. We were so terrified of the gentile students that during recess, when we had to leave the classroom, we went to the washroom and hid until the bell rang. It was the only way we could think of to avoid the constant abuse.

My brother, Ivan, who was then eight years old, would wait for me outside the school every day so that we could run home together. One day, I came out and he wasn't there. I was terrified and searched frantically for him. I finally found him by the post office, where some students had pulled off his pants and started kicking him. I was able to drag him away from them since I was almost twelve years old and much stronger than his fellow students. The months that we were in this degrading school environment were hell.

I came home from that horrible school one day to find a Hungarian peasant sitting in our kitchen, waiting for my father. He told my father that he had been sent from Levice to take me back with him to my grandmother's place. Many Slovakian Jews had escaped to Hungary, of which Levice was now a part, for safety. My grandmother had sent all the necessary documents for me to cross the border. I was elated, but my father gave the messenger some money and food and said, "Tell my mother-in-law that I appreciate her efforts, but Agi is my daughter and she will stay with me. If we survive, she will survive." I broke down, completely dejected. I know now, however, that if my father had let me go, which I so desperately wanted, I would have died two years later with my grandmother in Auschwitz. She perished in the concentration camp with all her sisters and their families in 1944.[5]

In 1942, the local authorities in Bardejov recommended that the remaining seven Jewish families in Bardejov convert to Christianity in order to remain there safely. Even though I had not been brought up in a religious environment, I didn't want to convert because I knew that my mother was buried in a Jewish cemetery. My father couldn't convince me, so he took me to see my schoolmate's mother, Dr. Elisabeth Grosswirth. Dr. Grosswirth put pressure on me to convert, telling me that if I didn't, I would be putting my whole family in danger.

A Protestant priest volunteered to help the remaining families go through their conversion – he would convert the parents first and, a few days later, all their children. Doing this would ensure that the baptismal documents showed that the parents were already Protestants when their children converted. Unfortunately, in my case, only my father would be identified as Protestant; my mother would still be identified as a Jew. On the day of our conversion, eighteen Jewish children went to the church, among them our friend Dr. Robert Zeman. Within an hour, we had all been converted.

Time passed quickly and our life went on. Then, in April 1944, the Red Army advanced toward eastern Poland, attempting to reach the Dukla Pass, a mountain pass on the border between Poland and Slovakia.[6] The fact that they were close led the authorities to decide

---

5   Hungary was allied with Nazi Germany during World War II, but until 1944 was not occupied and did not implement severe anti-Jewish measures. On March 19, 1944, Germany occupied Hungary and by April had forcibly confined 500,000 Jews to ghettos. Mass deportations soon began and by July 1944, 440,000 Hungarian Jews had been deported to Auschwitz. Over 1,000 Jews were deported to Auschwitz from Levice, where Agnes's grandmother lived.

6   See the map on page xxx–xxxi. Following the defeat of the German army at Stalingrad in February 1943, Soviet offensives advanced steadily westward, liberating most of Russia, Belorussia, the Ukraine and, by the spring of 1944, advancing into eastern Poland.

to evacuate the civil population of Bardejov, excluding working men, to central Slovakia. Included were the few remaining Jewish (now converted) families.

My father secured accommodations for our family in Liptovské Kľačany, in the middle of Slovakia, very close to the Low Tatra Mountains. In a few days, we packed all our belongings and travelled the almost three hundred kilometres to Kľačany by train. My father accompanied Ivan and me, along with my stepmother and step-grandmother. After getting us settled, he had to return to Bardejov but promised to visit us every two weeks. After he left, I felt completely lost.

Kľačany was a lovely, colourful Protestant village of less than a thousand. The villagers didn't know that we were Jewish, so life was far easier than it had been in Bardejov. There were other Jewish evacuees in the village but, like us, they all pretended to be Christian.

We didn't have to go to school in April – it was closed because of the unstable situation – so we played with the other village children. Among them was a boy named George Komar, the son of the local notary. I was almost fourteen at that time; he was sixteen and very attracted to me. In this part of Slovakia, when a boy was in love, it was customary for him to put up a tree with colourful decorations. He would place this tree – called a May Tree – in front of the girl's house. On May 1 – May Day – I awoke to see a beautiful tree in front of my window. I was so surprised; I had never heard of such a custom, nor did I know the meaning of it. My father had just arrived for a visit and was very proud of me, exclaiming, "You're such a big girl already." George came and introduced himself to my parents and invited us to his house for a festive dinner. It was quite an honour because the Komar family was the most prestigious in the village.

On August 29, 1944, Slovak anti-Nazi resisters began an uprising against the Germans and the collaborationist government of Slovakia and a revolt broke out in central Slovakia. Within forty-eight hours the uprising was defeated, although the battle in central Slovakia continued for two more months. The Germans eventually took over the government and the country completely. That was the end of our easier times.

Living in the Forest

October 26, 1944, was a cool, rainy day in Kľačany. I was playing with my skipping rope when all of a sudden I heard my stepmother screaming that we had to run. We could hear bombs exploding in the distance. I panicked; everybody around me, including villagers with their cattle, began running to the forest. Instead of going inside for my warm coat, I grabbed only Ivan's hand. My stepmother and step-grandmother followed and we ran deep into the forest.[1]

We met Slovak partisans in the forest who told us that the villagers could return home, but that the Jews should stay.[2] The partisans forced open a cottage and told the women and children to go in. We were wet, tired, hungry and pressed together like sardines. I fell asleep and had a dream in which I saved our family. I dreamt about my little green room in Bardejov, where it was nice and warm. I wanted to go into my room through a cold corridor when somebody

---

1 The bombs that Agnes and her family heard were part of the Soviet invasion of Slovakia that started at the Dukla Pass on September 8, 1944, and reached the lower Tatras area in late October. This area was the site of intense fighting between Soviet and German troops until November 1944.

2 The partisans in central Slovakia were groups comprised of Slovak political dissidents, Jews, army deserters and Soviet prisoners of war. For more information on partisans, see the glossary.

grabbed my shoulder. It was a woman dressed like a nun and she told me not to go into my warm room, but to stay in the cold corridor. I asked, "Who are you to tell me such nonsense?" She replied, "I am your mother and I am watching over you." I opened my eyes and felt my stepmother's hands shaking my shoulder. She was shouting at me, "Wake up! It's already dark outside. Grandmother wants to go back into the village and we have to join the other people who are going back." I told her about my dream. A lady by the name of Mrs. Erdelyi was listening and said, "Sarolta, it is an omen. Don't go back. We are staying too – let's all stay until the morning." My stepgrandmother was furious, calling my dream ridiculous. "Instead of going to my bed," she argued, "I have to stay in this horrible place?"

We later heard that some of the Jews who had returned to Kľačany had been shot by the German soldiers who were guarding the entry into the valley. If not for my dream, we would all have died. My stepmother was very grateful for my dream and told everybody after the war about this story. For me, this incident confirmed for me what I had always known – that my darling mother was, is and always will be watching over me.

It turned out that my father had foreseen difficulties ahead. During one of his visits from Bardejov, he told me and Ivanko a huge secret. He had brought four brushes for clothes-cleaning with him, and embedded inside the brushes were plates of twenty-four-carat dental gold. Should it become necessary, we were to use the gold to save our lives. Fortunately, my stepmother had taken them with her when we escaped into the forest.

The morning after my dream, we were woken up by a very loud explosion. The partisans advised us to run even deeper into the forest because the German soldiers were getting closer. The villagers had already built several underground bunkers to sell to the Jewish refugees. My stepmother gave the first brush filled with gold as payment for our family to have accommodations in one of the bunkers. Several other Jewish families – including four members of the Svarin family, the five Landesmanns, the five Lippas, the five Erdelyis, and some other families – shared our bunker.

A total of twenty-nine people were crammed into a very small space. The bunker was camouflaged into the terrain so as not to be visible from the outside. It was approximately three metres by five metres. It had hardly any ventilation, just a small door that could be opened to get in and out. We slept on wooden bunk beds squeezed tightly together. We had no food supply. The first three days, when we had no food at all, Ivanko found a piece of bacon skin that had probably been thrown out by forest labourers. He and I chewed on it for two days. We melted snow for water, so at least we weren't thirsty. After three days, we found horses frozen in the forest. The partisans had brought the horses with them from the uprising, but since they couldn't feed them, they left them to freeze to death. Horsemeat was a huge luxury. Villagers often brought potatoes to the bunkers – which they sold to us at a very high price – and they also brought us a steel kettle so that we could cook inside the bunker on an open fire, which was also our only source of heat. Women cooked on the open fire once a day and everybody got a small portion of the food.

Not far from us was a larger bunker that was the headquarters of the partisan military unit. A doctor from the partisan headquarters warned us of the danger of a typhus outbreak and, therefore, to not use unclean melted snow for drinking water. We went out to look around and found several other bunkers containing Jews scattered around the forest within approximately fifteen minutes walking distance from each other. After a few days of confusion, rules had to be established for the cohabitation of so many people, and a leader, Frankl from Prešov, was chosen to represent all the Jews. A number of rules were set, including one that three times a day we had to bring water for cooking and drinking from a creek fifteen minutes away.

Because we didn't have our father with us, all this work was piled up on me. My stepmother, who was thirty-eight at the time, declared that she and her mother were too old to do such hard work. Ivanko was only ten, so it was left to me, at fourteen, to go with the rest of the men from the bunker to bring water and wood for cooking and heating.

We were still able to maintain contact with the villagers and they would let us know whenever the Germans pulled out of the village for a few days. This gave us an opportunity to bring some bread, potatoes and apples from the village. It was my responsibility to go with the men on this three-hour walk to the village. I continued to do this throughout the bitterly cold winter from October to March. I also had to carry the very heavy load of food to the bunker on my back. My stepmother never offered to go in my place. When the people from the bunker said to her, "You should go instead of this child," her excuse was that if the Germans caught her, her dark colouring made it more likely that they would suspect that she was Jewish.

During my first expedition, I went to our previous apartment to bring back a goose-feather duvet to help ease the frigid temperatures at night. My family was delighted that I had brought it back, but I never got to enjoy it. They covered themselves, not leaving enough of the duvet for me. I cried, asking my own mother to save me. The other people in our bunker were outraged at my stepmother's behaviour, and promised me that if we survived the war, they would tell my father what happened.

Every day we suffered from lice, hunger and cold. One day, as usual, I went with the men to get water. We would always see fresh footprints in the snow from the neighbouring bunker, but on this particular day, I saw only my friend Alice from one of the other bunkers, and no other footprints. The adults I was walking with said, "Maybe they're still sleeping." At noon, when we went out for the second time, we noticed there were still no footprints, so we went to see what was going on. The sight that greeted us was the most horrific I've ever seen: the doors to the bunker were open, and approximately ten feet from the bunker were the dead bodies of the families living there – sixteen children, parents and grandparents, who had probably been killed the evening before. All the bodies were already covered with snow.

In a panic, we ran from the bunker to the partisan headquarters. The partisans knew that the military gangs operating under the direction of former Red Army general Andrei Vlasov, who collaborated with the Germans, had committed many similar atrocities, and thought that this may have been some of his work.[3] Now we knew that we had additional enemies among us and relied on the partisans to protect us. Among them were a few Jewish partisans who didn't disclose their origins because of the strong antisemitism among their Slovak group. These undercover Jewish partisans came to the bunkers to help us. They wanted to supply us with handguns for protection against Vlasov's forces, but none of the seven adult men from our bunker knew how to handle a gun. Instead, two men stood on guard every night. If they suspected any danger, one of them would run to the headquarters. It was a harrowing time.

During our weekly routine walk to the village, I had the best contact of all – the Komar family. George's mother was extremely good to me. I came to her every week and she always cleaned me of lice, prepared food for me and let me bathe in their house. She filled my backpack, gave me apples and even accompanied me to the edge of the forest. From there, I had to walk with the other men for the three hours it took to get back to our bunker. When I returned from the village with my backpack, I handed over all the food to my stepmother. I was so exhausted that I immediately fell asleep. By the time I woke up, all the food was gone – I often cried with hunger. When the people in the bunker got upset with my stepmother, she would simply say, "She eats at the Komars' place."

----

3 Soviet General Andrei Vlasov began collaborating with German forces in 1942 while in captivity in Germany, where he founded the Russian Liberation Army, an anti-Communist, pro-German force, directing Soviet soldiers who had defected and organizing them to fight Red Army partisans.

On December 5, 1944, the Jewish partisans went to all the Jewish bunkers to warn us that the other partisans were preparing liquor and the next day – December 6, St. Nicholas Day – were planning to bring all the young Jewish girls from the bunkers to their headquarters to have a good time. The girls' parents decided to send their daughters into the village to get them out of harm's way. I remember my stepmother asking one of the Jewish partisans what he thought of me, whether I was just a child or a grown woman, and whether she should send me to the village with the other girls. I remember his answer very clearly. He said, "She is a beautiful young girl. It will be safer to send her with the rest of the girls."

The next morning, three girls from our bunker, and six from the other bunkers, headed into the village. I went straight to the Komar family, and as usual they gave me a warm and friendly welcome. The other girls went to different people whom they knew. I had only been there for an hour when Mr. Komar came running into the kitchen and exclaimed, "We have to hide you in the attic. The Germans are searching every house and they have already caught many of the girls." It was a terrifying feeling to be hidden in a haystack in the attic, waiting to see if the Germans would find me. But because Mr. Komar was the notary, his house wasn't searched nearly as thoroughly as the other houses. Unfortunately, the Germans caught five of the nine girls, including one from our bunker, Renee Lippa from Ružomberok.

Just before dusk, the Komars took me down to their kitchen, kissed me, filled my backpack and took me to the edge of the valley. From there I walked alone for three hours, in complete darkness, toward my bunker. When I arrived, they already knew about the tragedy. Everybody was crying. Some of the girls had returned, but the Jewish partisans had told them that the five who had been captured had been deported to concentration camps.

After this terrible event, our situation began to deteriorate. Elderly people and infants began to die off because of the poor hygiene, malnutrition, paratyphoid fevers and pneumonia. In addition to these tragedies, the outlook for our liberation seemed hopeless: there had been no progress on the battlefield for a month. Life was almost unbearable; many people gave up and went back to town, where they risked being deported to concentration camps.

But our life went on. I picked up water three times a day, collected wood once a week and brought food to my family for a whole week at a time. I was lucky to have the Komar family, who filled my backpack every time I visited, never forgetting to put in four apples, our only source of vitamins. After the war, I went back to visit these generous people to thank them for their kindness and bravery, for risking their own lives to help save mine.

Once, while returning from the Komars with food, I passed a bunker where three brothers and their families, including infants and children, lived. Just two days before, one of the babies had died from diarrhea. They knew that I had apples and begged me to leave them for their children. I left them all four of my apples and returned to our bunker, where my stepmother and stepgrandmother immediately began searching my bag. They asked me where the apples were and, when I told them that I had given them to the families in the Mezey bunker because their children were dying, they both began to scream at me, pushing me out of the bunker, demanding that I get the apples back. As usual, the other people in our bunker defended me, telling my stepmother to go at least once to pick up the food, instead of attacking me and pulling my hair.

Near the end of February, Ivan got an extremely high fever and developed a large swelling full of pus under his armpit. He was seriously ill. Everybody agreed that he should be taken to the village to see a doctor. The partisans gave me instructions that if the Germans caught us, we should say that we were children from east Slovakia, evacuees who had lost our parents. In this situation, we again thought that it was safer for me to go with him into the village rather than my stepmother.

I walked for three hours with my poor little brother, whose fever was so high that he wanted to give up several times. I had to pull him by his hands to keep him going. It was afternoon by the time we found the local doctor. We knocked at the window and his wife opened the door. I told her we were evacuees who had lost our parents and that my little brother was very sick. After she had taken us into his office, the doctor came in and found Ivan half unconscious. He took his temperature and then looked at his swollen armpit. It took him twenty minutes to sterilize his instruments and during that time Ivan fell asleep on the examination table. Without any notice, the doctor cut open Ivan's armpit and an unbelievable amount of pus came out. Ivan's condition changed immediately – his fever dropped and the pain subsided completely. I had never seen anything like it. I don't even remember if I asked the doctor how much I owed him.

The doctor took us into the kitchen, gave us hot milk, bread and butter, and told us that he knew we were Jewish children who had probably come from the forest. His wife packed us some food and accompanied us to the edge of the valley. The doctor gave Ivan some painkillers and a Thermos bottle of hot milk. He and his wife both said, "God bless you, children, take care," and Ivan and I almost started to cry because of their goodness. It was nearly dark when we got back to our bunker. Everyone had been waiting for us, and they were all impressed to see Ivan so happy and well, with no pain and no fever, and to hear how compassionate the doctor and his wife had been.

On March 9, 1945, our leader, Frankl, was summoned to the partisan headquarters and told that all the partisans were leaving the valley for Brezno nad Hronom, where the Red Army had already liberated the area. The Soviets had halted their advance close to us, but we were encircled by the German army. Now we couldn't even get to the village for food.

The partisans told Frankl that the only way to get to Brezno nad Hronom was by an exceedingly dangerous and long route along the crests of the Low Tatra Mountains, and they could not take responsibility for the safety of the children, elderly and sick people among us.

The Germans were still stationed in the villages and holding strong. The partisans said that they were leaving the next day, early in the morning. Frankl would have to decide our fate, whether we would stay or follow them.

After Frankl's discussions with the partisans, we all gathered outside. I remember to this day the speech that he gave, warning us that if we chose to go, our lives would be in danger. The mountains were over two thousand metres high and we would have to climb to the peaks, where the paths were narrow and the ice was extremely slippery. One single misstep would mean certain death. There was an understandable amount of panic. We wondered what to do: should we stay without food or access to the village, or face new danger?

Our leader proclaimed that he and his family of two children and a grandmother were going to leave with the partisans. Approximately 120 of the people from our group of 180 gathered early the next morning to join them. Among us were two elderly ladies – the sons of one of them, Mrs. Svarin, carried her in a blanket. It was heartbreaking to watch. We lined up, one after the other. We had to follow the partisans along the crest of the mountains and no one was allowed to stop. At around three o'clock in the afternoon, after an eight-hour walk without any breaks, we arrived at a mountain called Solisko, at an elevation of 2,400 metres. The elderly people and children received some soup and potatoes. The rest of the adults were given something hot to drink.

The partisans prepared lots of tents on a closed plateau, where we slept until early the next morning. Then we followed them to Magurka, which was just over 1,000 metres high and was another seven-hour walk. We arrived without having had any food, but were given the same limited amount of nourishment that we had received on Solisko.

That evening, hundreds of Jews – those who had been hiding in the same region as us – gathered together and were warned that the most dangerous trip lay ahead of us. We would have to climb

Chabenec, which was steep, rocky and narrow, the peak of which was almost 2,000 metres high. The partisans told us that the weather could change within an hour to a terrible snowstorm, as it had earlier that day. The weather had been beautiful when we left, but had quickly turned nightmarish. A number of people had slipped on the steep, icy mountain path and fallen to their deaths.

We had to decide whether to continue. We were all exhausted, hungry and cold. We couldn't sleep and we didn't know what to do. I asked for guidance from my mother, but unfortunately I didn't dream about her. My stepmother asked me what to do. I told her that although I was unsure, I felt that we should go on. Many people decided to stay and face the unknown, but we lined up in the morning to follow the partisans.

It was a beautiful, sunny winter day. The walkway was only two feet wide, and both sides of the mountain were icy and steep, so we lined up in a strict formation. One wrong step meant certain death. Ivanko held my coat from behind. Both sides of the slopes were littered with dead bodies. We saw mothers with their children, frozen in a locked embrace. They looked as if they were still alive, but they were frozen with their eyes open. I also remember seeing dead, frozen partisans who had slipped from the path. I will never forget this frightening sight.

Luckily, there was no wind – the weather was sunny and calm. God and my dear mother were with us. We walked for nine hours until we came to a new valley where we saw a sign that read, "The Soviets have liberated the next village." In another three hours – the time it would take to walk to the village of Hel'pa – we would finally achieve our liberation. It was March 12, 1945. We were overjoyed, crying from sheer happiness. In the middle of our celebration a partisan came to warn us that we could be falling into a trap and that we needed to be cautious. He said there could still be Germans in the village instead of the Soviets. A huge panic broke out. We were hungry and completely exhausted. We couldn't stand on our feet anymore so we sat down on the icy snow. Our disappointment and despair lifted when a young, Jewish couple from Poland whom we had never met before volunteered to explore the village to find out the truth. They told us to be patient for another five hours, and that if they had not returned within that time, it meant that they had been captured by the Germans.

The moonlight was bright and we were all falling asleep. Everybody made sure to wake each other often because of the danger of freezing to death. The brave Polish couple arrived back at around one o'clock in the morning, crying, "We are liberated!" It was an unbelievably euphoric moment. We didn't feel tired or hungry anymore and we walked the three hours through the valley to Heľpa, where Soviet soldiers were stationed. When we arrived, the adults and elderly people all kissed the soldiers' hands in gratitude.

The next day, the Red Army soldiers sheltered us in an empty school and gave us food. Everybody slept for hours. I couldn't believe that I was finally free. But I still felt lost without my father and all I could think about was finding him. We hadn't been in contact with him for seven months and we had no idea whether he was even alive. I prayed and asked my dear mother to keep him safe.

Starting Life Again

When we awoke in the school in Heľpa, we felt that we had had the most luxurious sleep in our lives. Although we were sleeping on straw, it was heavenly in comparison to the bare wood in the bunkers. We were told that we would be taken to Brezno nad Hronom, which had already been established as a centre for refugees run by several relief organizations, including the United Nations Relief and Rehabilitation Administration and the Swiss Red Cross. Our first stop was the de-lousing facilities, as we were badly infested with lice. They took away our clothes and replaced them with clean serviceable ones.

After our first cleansing stop, we were taken to a big school equipped with comfortable bunk beds. We went out to feast on a hearty meal, which we greatly appreciated. After we ate, my step-mother and stepgrandmother wanted to return to the school, but I refused. I told them that I wanted to leave Heľpa and look for my father. They were both furious with me, but I didn't care. Ivanko declared that he was going to go with me, leaving his mother and grandmother behind. I asked him not to, but he insisted, so I agreed to take him.

There was no easy method of transportation; the only vehicles on the roads were Soviet military trucks and we were at their mercy as to whether they would take us or not. The first military truck I stopped was already carrying lots of civilians and I asked where they were going. They told us that they were heading to Prešov, which is only about thirty-five kilometres from Košice, so I knew that we would be going in the right direction. The Soviet driver had stopped for us because we were children – I didn't realize then how lucky it was that I was short and looked so young. I found out later that Red Army soldiers had raped many young girls. I was three months shy of my fifteenth birthday.

We arrived in Prešov in the early evening and found out that similar relief organizations were operating there. We followed the other civilians to a local school, where we found accommodation and food. We slept there overnight and the next morning, after getting some food, I started trying to flag down a military truck. It took a while, but I finally found one that was going to Raslavice, a village that was only about twenty-five kilometres from Bardejov, and asked the driver to take us there.

Once we had arrived in Raslavice we stood at the side of the road until we saw a villager approaching in a horse-drawn carriage. He asked where we were going and when I told him that we were trying to get to Bardejov, he said, "Get on." Within an hour we had arrived in Bardejov. We thanked the villager and jumped out of the carriage.

It took me a long time to realize that I didn't have to hide anymore, that I was free. Seeing Bardejov after five months of hiding in the bunkers and dreaming about it was unreal. Everything looked strange to me. We didn't know where to go. I went to the parish church where we had been converted to ask if they knew whether my father had survived. The priest and his wife there were extremely nice to us and very moved that we had come. They gave us the best news I could have hoped for – my father was alive and had gone to Poprad, about seventy-five kilometres away in the centre of Slovakia, to try to find us. They served us food that we had only dreamt about and also offered their home to us until we could find our father, but I had a gentile friend, Eva Korinkova, with whom I felt more comfortable. We told the priest's wife that we would come back if Eva wasn't home. We thanked them for giving us the best news, food and love, and headed toward Eva's house. She and her family were at home and overjoyed to see that we were alive. They told us that they had met our father five days earlier and he had told them that he was going to look for his family. They insisted that we stay with them until my father returned.

After three days of sleeping in a normal bed, we were still very groggy when my father, stepmother and stepgrandmother arrived. I started to cry with excitement, seeing my father alive, but could see immediately that he wasn't pleased with me. My heart almost broke in two and I asked him, "Aren't you happy to see me?" "Yes, I am very happy that you're alive," he replied. "Jewish partisans in Poprad told me that you had been caught by the Germans on December 6, and that only the rest of the family had survived. But I'm not happy with your behaviour, how difficult you were in the bunker. On top of everything, you took Ivan away with you and left your stepmother and stepgrandmother worrying about you." Hearing this from him was almost too much to bear.

My father then told us how he had survived. He had been working in Bardejov until December 1944. One day, in the middle of work, a friend of his, Father Zidishin, an Orthodox Catholic priest, burst into his office and said, "Leave everything as it is, I have a horse and carriage waiting in front of your office. I'll take you to my parish and on the way we'll pick up Mr. and Mrs. Risa Atlas." Mrs. Atlas was a pharmacist who had a son my age. The priest explained that he had found out that all the Jewish exemptions were going to be annulled the next day and the Jews were going to be killed. The priest drove them to his parish, which was thirty-six kilometres from Bardejov, and hid my father and the Atlases in his pig stall during the day; at night he hid them in his cellar and gave them proper food.

The Soviet army liberated Bardejov on January 20, 1945, and arrived at the nearby village soon afterward. All the villagers had to assemble at the main square – the men of the village were all serv-

ing in the military, so only the women, the priest and my father remained. At that time, my father was a young man of forty-four, which
made the Soviet commander very suspicious. "Why are you here?" he
shouted at my father. Terrified, my father answered, "I am a Jew. I was
hidden at this priest's house." The commander started to cry and embraced him, saying, "I came all the way from Moscow and have seen
only dead Jews. You are the first one I've seen alive." His name was
Captain Zaretsky and he kept in touch with my father for many years.

We started our new life. Our old house had been taken over by
someone else, so we moved to a house that had belonged to the Singer
family who, sadly, never came back from the camps. Dr. Singer had
been a veterinarian, and his wife and her twin sister were artists. They
drew the family portrait that I have in my bedroom. The two sisters
– we called them Tante (Aunt) Elsa and Tante Fritzi – also taught
English and German.

I have to tell you a funny story from before we went into hiding. I
took private German lessons from Tante Fritzi and on one occasion,
she was preparing minced meat while she was teaching me and, in
the middle of her work, she had to leave to talk to somebody. I was
left alone with the minced meat and started to taste it. I liked it very
much and by the time she came back, I had eaten all the raw meat.
Tante Fritzi was a very intelligent woman – instead of yelling at me,
she explained that I was now in danger of getting an intestinal parasite from the uncooked meat and made me conjugate *der Bandwurm*,
which in German means parasite. These two wonderful ladies and
the veterinarian, Tante Elsa's husband, perished in the Holocaust.

We moved into their beautiful home, a two-storey house with a
garden that was very close to the centre of town. We had our three-
bedroom apartment on the ground floor and my father opened his
dental office on the second floor. My father gradually got back a lot of
the furniture, paintings and carpets, as well as the grand piano, that
had been hidden in the houses of his gentile friends.

Our lives had seemingly gone back to normal, but psychologically

I couldn't accept the fact that many of my Jewish friends who had been deported never returned. I later discovered that most of them had perished in the concentration camps. My closest friend, Magda, however, did come out of hiding – she and her family had also been living in a bunker in the woods under circumstances that were similar to ours. We were thrilled to see each other. Another girlfriend of mine, Vera Grosswirth, also returned. It took me several months to adjust to the fact that I could move around the town freely and play in the park.

The war was not quite over and the schools were still closed. My father eventually decided I should be in Grade 10 but, because I hadn't been at school for most of the last three years, he hired a private teacher to tutor me. His name was Ivanco and he later became the dean of the medical faculty in Košice. He hadn't been a friend of the Jews during the war – he had been generally antisemitic – but he did help me as a tutor after the war.

My strained relationship with my stepmother and my stepgrandmother continued. It wasn't easy but I simply learned to deal with their abusive behaviour. My father was heavily involved in his work and didn't have a close relationship with me either. My only close family tie was with Ivanko, who was always on my side. I still held on to some hope that my maternal grandmother, Uncle Jozko, and the rest of the family were looking for me, but mostly I felt despondent and helpless. To distract myself, I concentrated on preparing for my upcoming exams and spent time with Magda, Vera and some of my non-Jewish friends.

Finally, on May 9, 1945, World War II came to an end in Europe, and most of the world, other than the fascists and their collaborators – there were plenty of them in Bardejov – celebrated. Toward the end of May, I was sitting at the window when, suddenly, I couldn't believe what I was seeing. I thought it was a dream. My dearest uncle Jozko appeared before me! I shouted for joy and ran to him. He had a little suitcase with him. He put it down on the sidewalk, grabbed me in his arms and started to cry, telling me that I had grown into a fine young lady. I was almost fifteen years old and he hadn't seen me since I was eight. My father was in his office and his windows were open, so he could hear my sobbing. When he came down and saw Jozko lift me into his arms, he was thrilled that another member of our family had survived. He invited Jozko to come into the house, where he was greeted by my stepmother and stepgrandmother.

I asked Jozko right away about my grandmother and the rest of the family. He took me onto his lap and started to cry. "Out of our entire family, probably only your uncle, my brother Bandi in Palestine, is alive." He asked if I remembered his cousin Pali Knapp and his wife, Bronka. They too had survived, but nobody else from my mother's family had come back. I jumped off his lap and ran away to cry in private. I ended up in our garden where our dog, Cesar, was tied up. I freed him and clung to him as I continued to weep.

I overheard my uncle telling my family to leave me alone. I don't know how long I was there, but after a while Uncle Jozko came to me. "Agika, I know that you are unhappy here. Right now I'm staying with Pali and Bronka, but I promise you that as soon as I settle down on my own, I will come for you. You will live with me and I will care for you the same way your grandmother would if she were still alive. You will attend school in Levice and in time you will be happy again." I kissed Uncle Jozko, thanked him and told him that I was sorry but I had to go to sleep after hearing such shocking news. Jozko stayed with us for three days and I spent almost every moment with him. I finally told him that I had known since the age of seven that my mother had died. He told me lots of stories about my family in Levice.

Jozko asked my father if he could take me to Košice to see my mother's grave and my father agreed. My father wouldn't go with us because it would be considered disrespectful to his marriage to Sarolta. Košice was only eighty-five kilometres from Bardejov, but it took a whole day to get there because transportation was still so difficult. When Jozko and I arrived at my dear mother's grave, we wept together. At that moment, I accepted her death.

We stayed at the cemetery for quite a long time and lit candles as Jozko spoke to his sister. "My dear Katka," he said, "I have brought you your little daughter. Guard over her." That made me cry even more. With heavy hearts, we kissed the tombstone and left. It was late at night when we got back to Bardejov. Jozko slept over at my father's house and the next day I accompanied him to the railway station. I felt so protected when I was with him. I believed in his promise that he would take me to his home. I felt secure for the first time in a long time.

In September 1945, I passed the Grade 9 exams so that I could go into Grade 10. My girlfriend Magda was also accepted into the same grade, but Vera Grosswirth, who had been my classmate before the war, fell one year behind. It was odd to finally be equal to my gentile classmates. There were many boys in my high school, but only seven girls. It was a new school year, a new beginning for me, and I gradually adjusted to what was a normal school environment. I attribute this to my healthy and positive outlook on life. I was quite happy, enjoying what life had to offer.

When I got home from school one day, my father called me into his room. To my surprise, I saw none other than Mr. Landesmann, a man who had lived in the same forest bunker as me and my family. He told my father that he wanted to keep the promise he had made to me and tell my father how I had been treated by my stepmother and stepgrandmother. In front of Mr. Landesmann, my father asked me to tell him what had really gone on in that bunker during the war. I was terrified because my stepmother knew that this visit was going to happen at some point, and had warned me, back in the bunker, that if I told the truth, I would ruin my father and stepmother's marriage and God would punish me by taking my brother away from me. I didn't know what to do so I replied, "I forget and I didn't behave well either. I ran away with Ivan after the war, and made them worry." At that point Mr. Landesmann only caressed my head and said to me, "I feel very sorry for you. If you were my daughter and somebody treated you the way you were treated, I wouldn't live with such a person." He left the room without shaking my father's hand.

After Mr. Landesmann left, my father asked me again what had really happened. I was so superstitious that I really was afraid that God would punish me if I told the truth. I repeated what I had told Mr. Landesmann and that was the end of our discussion.

Soon after Mr. Landesmann's difficult visit, however, we received some very good news about an impending visit from my father's brother Sanyi, along with his daughter Katka. Uncle Sanyi had survived the Holocaust in a labour camp, but his wife, Jolan, and his younger daughter, Evike, had perished in Auschwitz. Katka, who had been eighteen at the time, had managed to survive in the camp.[1] After learning what had happened to his wife and young daughter, Uncle Sanyi had fallen into a deep depression and stopped talking completely. He lived in his own world and didn't react to any discussions, so we thought that he didn't understand anything that was going on around him. My father was very understanding and loving toward him. He took him to a psychiatrist, who prescribed some medication, but nothing helped. Even Katka's presence didn't make any difference. After a few weeks of staying with us, though, Katka could no longer tolerate my stepmother's behaviour toward me and left for Budapest, where Joska, my father's eldest brother, had survived the war with his family. Her father didn't even react to her departure.

Fortunately, most of my father's family had escaped the brutality of the Nazis and their collaborators. His parents had died of natural causes in Lučenec before the war, and his youngest brother, Dezso,

---

1   Upon arrival at Auschwitz, prisoners underwent a "selection" process, whereby those deemed unfit for work, most often children, the sick and the elderly, were sent to their death in the gas chambers, while the rest were forced to work as slave labourers.

had died in a tragic accident there at the age of twenty-one. Of his remaining three siblings, as I've said, the eldest, Joska, survived in Budapest with his whole family and Sanyi and his daughter Katka survived the camps. My father's only sister, Aranka, had married in Romania before the war and emigrated to Palestine.

Every day when I came home from school, I kissed Uncle Sanyi's balding head as he sat constantly eating at the kitchen table with his head bowed down. One day, when I arrived home from school, my stepmother shouted at me, "Go to the store immediately and bring back ten bottles of mineral water because our maid forgot to bring it." I put down my schoolbag, took the empty bottles and asked her for money. When I also asked her if I could bring only five bottles because they were quite heavy, she started pulling my hair and beating me with the empty bottles. To everyone's surprise, the previously unresponsive Sanyi jumped up from his seat and started slapping her face. Sarolta began to shriek. My father came down from his office in the middle of this commotion and, not quite believing his eyes, stopped Sanyi from hitting his wife. Sanyi broke his long silence to say, "I don't want to stay here any longer. I cannot stand witness to the abuse of your poor daughter." Although he didn't leave right away, that was nonetheless a turning point in his life. From that day on, I loved Uncle Sanyi even more than I had before.

A few months after this incident, Katka returned from Budapest to introduce us to her fiancé, Frici, with whom she was very much in love. She was overjoyed to see the change in her father. My father opposed Katka's decision to marry Frici, but gave up trying to convince her to change her mind. Katka was a beautiful, sexy girl, and he felt that she would have many better opportunities in Bardejov. Katka remained firm in her decision and asked my father to arrange her wedding, which he did. My stepmother was Protestant – she had never changed her religion back to Judaism after her conversion – so the chuppah was at my friend Magda's house because they were

Orthodox.[2] The wedding dinner was at our house, though, and I helped out by serving. I had to carry three roasted ducks from the kitchen into the dining room and ended up slipping – all three ducks fell on the floor. No one noticed so I quickly picked them up and carried them into the dining room. I told everyone that I had an upset stomach so I wouldn't have to eat any of the duck.

I owned only one nightgown, which I gave to Katka as a wedding present. Katka and Frici would be spending their wedding night in my bedroom and, being a teenager, I was curious about what would happen there. So I deliberately left my schoolbag in my bedroom, giving me an excuse to go into the room while Katka and Frici were there. The newlyweds hollered at me to get lost, so I had to just grab my bag and leave.

After a few days, Katka and her new husband left and the psychiatrist who was treating Uncle Sanyi recommended that he start to engage in normal activity. He encouraged us to get him back to work, introduce him to a woman and help him carry on a normal life. My father arranged a job for him working as a sales representative for a dental supplier. He also got the address of a woman named Lotte Immergut, a widow in Košice with her own business, and introduced the two of them. The match turned out to be a great success and in three months they were married. In my opinion, they had a happy married life.

To my great joy, Uncle Jozko came back for a visit after three months to tell me that he was getting married. He wanted me to come to Levice for my summer vacation so that he could arrange my future.

The school year ended successfully and I was looking forward to getting away from Bardejov. But when I arrived in Levice in the

---

2   A chuppah is the canopy used in traditional Jewish weddings, usually made of a cloth (sometimes a prayer shawl) stretched or supported over four poles. It is meant to symbolize the home the couple will build together.

summer of 1946 at the age of sixteen, all my previous hopes for a life there were dashed. Bronka and Pali were still there, but almost every other house reminded me of relatives who had perished – it was as if the earth had swallowed them up. I experienced intense feelings of emptiness and pain. I missed my grandmother.

That summer I had a romance with a boy named Tomy Kaiser, who was in his first year of medical school at the University of Bratislava. He was my first love, but Uncle Jozko didn't approve of my relationship with him. His excuse was that Tomy's father was cheating on his wife, and that Tomy would do the same.

My new aunt, Ica, was very much in love with Uncle Jozko. She was a very tidy, hard-working person, but I sensed that she was jealous of me. She started to point out all my shortcomings to Jozko and I started to think that, much as I didn't want to, I should go back to live in Bardejov. I didn't want to disturb Jozko's new life with his wife, so I told him that I wanted to return to my school there. At the end of August, I went home to Bardejov.

Uncle Jozko and Aunt Ica soon had a baby girl, my new cousin Katka. I was thrilled at this new addition to our family, but after my first visit to see my little cousin in the summer of 1947, it was quite clear that I wasn't welcome there. Aunt Ica told me openly – though not in front of my uncle – that since Jozko now had his own daughter, I was old enough and smart enough to know that I should stay with my father.

After I returned from this visit, I started school in September and the new school year brought some interesting developments. For one thing, I fell in love with one of my schoolmates, Pali Marci. He was Hungarian and my high school principal's nephew. We had to meet in the cemetery because my father didn't approve of my having any romantic entanglements. Fortunately, though, the dead didn't disclose our innocent encounters.

I also experienced many hardships that school year. Two of the teachers at the school were openly antisemitic, which was very painful for me and Magda. We gradually built up our self-confidence and started to fight back. It was easier for us because we were both good students. The principal of the high school, Mr. Paul Dianishka, was my father's best friend. He secretly supported our fight because the antisemitic teachers were also anti-Hungarian, and his wife was Hungarian. The disappointments in my life had started to make me feel stronger – I wanted to fight against injustice, not only in my own life, but also in the wider community.

Many German collaborators had disappeared from our town for a while after the war and only later slowly started to return. With my new fighting spirit, I stood up to some of these people. One day, when I returned from school, I heard voices and could tell that my father and stepmother had some visitors. When I entered the room, to my amazement, I saw that Mr. and Mrs. Grofcik were engaging in a friendly conversation with my father – these were the antisemites who had had me and Magda thrown out of the football game all those years ago. I stood in shocked disbelief and told my father how Mrs. Grofcik had humiliated us. I shouted, "How could you let these devils into your house? I'm ashamed of you!" I ran into my room and slammed the door. My father and stepmother, instead of agreeing with me, punished me. My father told me, "I want to stay in Bardejov, and with your rebellious nature that you inherited from your mother's side, you are making our lives miserable. As long as you are living under my roof, I will not accept these kinds of scenes." I was devastated – I used to be so proud of my father, but this serious clash of opinions made me very disappointed in him. It was especially ironic because after the war my father had changed his name from Grossmann to Gonda because he decided that "Grossmann" sounded too German.

During that year, I realized that I didn't belong in either Bardejov or Levice, and I started making more regular visits to Uncle Sanyi and Aunt Lotte in Košice. Unlike my father, they were observant Jews, so I went there for the high holidays. Aunt Lotte took me to the synagogue and introduced me to some young Jewish students who belonged to a sizeable group of Hashomer Hatzair. I became close to two students in particular, Vera Spira and Imre Klein, among others. Zionist meetings were held once a month and I tried to be in Košice to participate in each of them. That summer, I went with them to a Moshava summer camp in the Súľovské skaly nature reserve in the mountains for two weeks.[3] It was a colourful, beautiful environment and I enjoyed spending time with my new friends. My father wasn't happy with my new orientation – he claimed that I acted in permanent opposition to him.

After the end of the school year, which I did very well in, I was rewarded with a three-week trip to a beautiful seaside resort in Kupari, Yugoslavia, with my friend Vera Grosswirth, accompanied by her aunt. As young eighteen-year-old girls, we had a wonderful time. I was quite successful with the opposite sex and had a very interesting encounter there. Vera and I were sitting on the terrace of a restaurant, with beautiful, romantic music playing in the background. A group of movie stars who had just finished filming a movie called *Majka* (Mother) were sitting close to us. One of the most handsome actors came to our table and asked Vera's aunt for permission to dance with me. I readily accepted. He had been doing film work in Prague, at a Barrandov film studio, for over a year, so he was able to speak to me in Czech.

From that day forward he was with us constantly and we began to fall in love. Vera's aunt felt responsible for me, so she tried to never leave me alone with him. Three days before we were due to leave, a funny thing happened. In front of Vera and her aunt, he declared

---

3 The Hebrew word *moshava* means settlement or village. Founded by the left-wing Zionist youth movement, *moshava* camps simulated life on a kibbutz – a cooperative, communal farming community in Palestine – while teaching campers about Judaism and socialism. For more information, also see the glossary entry for Hashomer Hatzair.

his love for me. He said he wanted to be with me permanently and proposed to me. Vera's aunt told him that our relationship couldn't be permanent since actors had a terrible reputation for not being able to stay in marriages. His response to this was to say, "I am sure that I love Agnesica so deeply that I could stay married to her for at least three years!" That was the end of my Yugoslavian love story.

On my way back to Bardejov from my fabulous vacation in Yugoslavia, I stopped in Levice to see Uncle Jozko and my cousin Katka. After I had been there for three weeks, I had a horrible dream in which I fell on the ground with all my teeth barely hanging on by a thread. When I woke up, I was shaking. I ran to see a woman who was very special to me, Mrs. Feldmann, to ask for her help in interpreting my dream. She had been a schoolmate of my mother's and really loved me. She had a son named Gyuri who was in his third year of medical school. He was very good- looking but had a dreadful nature. I almost agreed to marry him simply because I loved his mother so much – I felt strongly that I needed a mother more than I needed a good husband. Uncle Jozko knew why I wanted to marry Gyuri and told me that it would be the biggest mistake of my life to marry somebody for the wrong reason.

After hearing about my dream, Mrs. Feldmann told me that it was an extremely bad sign. As soon as I got back to my uncle's house, my aunt told me that a telegram had just arrived from my stepmother, asking me to go to Košice immediately because my father was gravely ill in hospital with a serious case of jaundice. He had been transferred there from Bardejov because the hospital in Košice was bigger and could offer better care. Gyuri took me to Zvolen, the nearest town to Sliač Airport.

When I arrived at the hospital in Košice, what I found was very distressing. When I walked into my father's room I didn't even recognize him. His whole body was yellow and he had lost a lot of weight. When he saw me, he started to cry. He said that he had to be transferred more than five hundred kilometres to a hospital in Prague because the hospital in Košice couldn't give him the care he needed either. I was so upset that I asked Uncle Sanyi to come with me to the cemetery to ask my mother to protect my father. I visited her grave every time I was in Košice.

The next day Ivan and my stepmother arrived and my father told me that his wife would be accompanying him to Prague. He had arranged for a young dentist, Tibor Valencik, to substitute for him at his office. School would be starting in just two weeks, but my father wanted me to put off going to school and take over the financial part of the office. If, by some miracle he recovered, I could start the school year late.

The scene at the railway station was traumatic. My father arrived by ambulance and was transferred into a sleeping car. Ivanko, Uncle Sanyi, Aunt Lotte and I waited, weeping, until the train pulled out of the station. That same day, Ivanko and I returned to Bardejov, where my stepgrandmother and our domestic help were waiting. This was the first time I felt that I needed to be mature and take charge of the whole family. The young dentist arrived and started to work in the office along with me. Every Sunday, I travelled to Košice and stopped over at Uncle Sanyi's house. Each time, he accompanied me to the cemetery, where I begged my mother for her help in returning my father to me.

Finding My Destiny

My last year of high school began, but I couldn't attend the lectures because I took my responsibilities to my father very seriously. After just over a month, my stepmother returned from Prague for a few days to pick up some money and delivered the devastating news that my father's prognosis was bleak. I was upstairs in my father's office when my stepmother called me into the bedroom where she was lying with her mother. "You're old enough to understand what we have to tell you," she announced. "Unfortunately, your father will not be coming back. My mother and I have decided that we are going to re-open her store in Prešov. You will have to stay with Uncle Jozko in Levice and decide about your future." I started to cry and told them that they were mistaken, that my father would recover. My mother would never permit this to happen, I thought, for me to be alone in this cruel world. I was shattered – I knew that I couldn't count on my uncle Jozko since he now had his own family to take care of.

Fortunately, my dear mother answered my prayers and my father returned to Bardejov with my stepmother at the beginning of October 1948. His recovery was miraculous, even for those famous doctors in Prague. I waited with Ivanko and my stepgrandmother at the train station, my heart pounding with pure joy and gratitude. When my father finally arrived and I went to embrace him, once again, I got the feeling that he wasn't pleased to see me. I couldn't understand it – he embraced Ivanko and his mother-in-law warmly but was very cold toward me. That night, I cried and wondered what could have happened. Did he want me to leave his house?

The next day my father spoke to me very formally, telling me that I was now free to return to school. I handed all the accounts and financial records over to him. I was too nervous to ask why he was so cold toward me. I had already asked my stepmother what was going on, but she had simply told me not to upset him with my questions, that he had his reasons and would tell me himself when he had recovered completely.

I went back to school a few days later. The first Sunday after my father's return, I went to the cemetery in Košice to thank my mother and ask her to help me out of this incomprehensible situation. I stopped by Uncle Sanyi's house afterward to talk to him. I had already told him about the fact that when my stepmother was certain that my father would die, she was ready to push me out of his house. This time, I told my uncle that when my father returned, he was not just cold toward me but completely estranged. Uncle Sanyi decided to come back to Bardejov with me to find out what was wrong with his brother. I didn't want him to come because I was worried about what would happen to my father if he got agitated, but Uncle Sanyi refused to be dissuaded. On the trip back to Bardejov he promised me that he would broach the subject gradually and calmly.

I couldn't concentrate at school the next day because I was too preoccupied with what was going on at home. To my surprise, when I got home my father was waiting in front of our house with Uncle Sanyi. He embraced me, sobbing, and told me why he had been disappointed in me. Apparently my stepmother had told him an enormous lie. She said that I had stolen money from the office and given it to Uncle Sanyi every Sunday. My uncle had explained to him that, yes, I had gone to Košice every Sunday, but not to bring him money. I had only come to pray at my mother's grave for my father's recovery. He had investigated the matter and told my father that his wife and mother-in-law had been planning to re-open their store in Prešov when my father died, and that they had taken the money and deposited it in a bank.

When my stepmother and stepgrandmother returned the deposit books they had taken from my father's dental office, my father could clearly see what had happened to the money. As a result of the confrontation between my father and my stepmother, my stepgrandmother was forced to leave the house and move to Bratislava to a Jewish seniors' home. She only stayed there five months before returning to Bardejov, though – my father had a soft heart and forgave her as well as his wife. He didn't want to cause complications at home. This whole episode confirmed for me once again that I would never really be able to find a home in either Bardejov or in Levice.

My father wasn't well enough to work in his dental office for about five months. The young dentist who was substituting for him, Tibor Valencik, was a good-looking young man from an aristocratic Hungarian family. He wanted to start a serious relationship with me and asked my father if he could invite his mother to our home to introduce me to her. She was a lovely person, from the highest society of Košice. My father was very much in favour of this relationship, especially because he thought that it would be advantageous to have a son-in-law working with him. This "ideal" relationship, however, was short-lived. One Sunday, Tibor invited me to a movie called *Ulica Graniczna* (Border Street). It was the tragic story of a little boy named David who lived in the Warsaw ghetto. It was so moving that I started crying as soon as the film started. Tibor was holding my hand during the show, but when the lights came on at intermission, he saw my tears and said dismissively, "How can you get so excited about a movie? It's very childish of you." I realized then and there that we had nothing in common – I needed someone whose background was more like mine and realized that I could probably never marry a gentile. I didn't explain any of this to him, though. I told him that I had to go right home, that I had forgotten that I still had some homework to do. When we arrived at the door to my house, I escaped to my room and locked the door behind me.

My father saw all of this happen. He talked to Tibor for a while and when the younger man had left, my father knocked on my door and asked me to justify my improper behaviour. When I explained the whole situation about the movie and Tibor's reaction, my father thought that I was just being silly and we had a huge argument. I remained adamant, however, that my relationship with Tibor was over and my father was really angry, refusing to accept how I felt. This was my breaking point. The following Sunday, I went to Košice to join a group that would be making aliyah to Israel with Hashomer Hatzair, the same group that I had been with at camp the previous summer.[1] Our departure was scheduled for November 1948, just a few months before my high school graduation.

After I had registered with the group, I returned to Bardejov and announced to my father that I would be leaving for Israel in five weeks. He got extremely upset and told me that he wouldn't force my relationship with Tibor, even though he felt that I was making a mistake. I had to promise him that I would finish high school, which at that time, was a significant achievement for a girl. He said that if I still wanted to go to Israel after graduation, he wouldn't stand in my way. I agreed that I should graduate before leaving, so he contacted the organization and cancelled my application for aliyah and I concentrated all my efforts into successfully finishing high school.

During the 1948–1949 school year there was a dramatic political development that affected our whole way of thinking – the Communist Party of Czechoslovakia seized control of the govern-

---

1 Aliyah, which in Hebrew means "ascent," is the term used to refer to the return of Jews to their historic homeland in Israel. During World War II and immediately afterward, Zionist groups worked to secure passage for Jewish refugees to British Mandate Palestine.

ment.[2] Although I never joined the party, Magda and I, as the only two Jewish girls in our class, sympathized with them. Communism was attractive to us, because, at least theoretically, it was a system that espoused the ideals of equality and social justice.

On May 27, 1949, I successfully graduated from high school. My father was very proud of me and encouraged me to submit an application to the faculty of medicine at Comenius University in Bratislava, the capital of Slovakia. About ten days after my graduation, my father and I went there so I could take the medical school admission examination and I was soon accepted into the program for the session beginning in September 1949.

We stayed in Bratislava for three days, during which my father arranged accommodations for me for the school year with the family of Ivan Kalina, a relative of my stepmother. Ivan, a well-known humourist who had published several books, was living in an apartment close to the university with his wife, daughter and mother. Because of his high status as an author, he was relatively well-off, so his apartment was large enough that I was to have my own room.

After completing all the necessary steps to get me started at the university, my father returned directly to Bardejov, while I stopped over at my uncle's house in Levice, which was only about 130 kilometres east of Bratislava on the way to Bardejov. Immediately after I arrived in Levice, a boy named Peter Kovac who was three years older than me began courting me. One of the reasons that so many boys were interested in me was that there weren't very many Jewish girls my age because so many had perished in concentration camps. Young men who were five or so years older than me – in their mid-

---

2 The Communist Party of Czechoslovakia, fully backed by the Soviet Union, won a majority of seats in the 1946 legislative elections, while the Democratic Party held the majority in Slovakia. Following two years of political tensions at both the national and regional level, the Communist Party first seized control of the Slovak National Council and, in February 1948, of the national parliament.

twenties – had returned from the camps ready to get married and were desperate to find a wife. On top of that, I must say that I was quite good-looking, educated and came from a respectable family.

Peter was very handsome, but Uncle Jozko, as he had in the past with others, opposed the relationship. He argued that Peter was too young and I was too immature. He said that he couldn't see any future in the match. I remember my aunt Ica saying to my uncle, "I don't know what's wrong with you, Jozko. Agi is a good-looking girl, but not extra special. Your reaction is always the same, that nobody is good enough for her." In spite of these arguments, I enjoyed spending time with Peter. Because we weren't allowed to be out together in the evenings (at that time, it was considered indecent for a young girl to go out for a social evening without a chaperone), we drove around on his new motorcycle during the day. One day, at the beginning of June, we went for a longer drive to a spa in Dudince, about twenty-five kilometres from Levice. On the way back it was raining, so the roads were slippery. Peter kept telling me to lean in the same direction as him, but I was so scared that I did exactly the opposite. The motorcycle ended up sliding out from under us and we both fell and injured ourselves. I suffered skin abrasions on both my thighs and my knees were bleeding, while Peter broke his leg. The motorcycle was also damaged. We weren't very far from Levice and a car stopped for us and took us to the hospital, where they examined us and gave us anti-tetanus shots. Peter's leg had to be put into a cast. He took me home in a taxi and didn't reproach me at all for my part in causing the accident. He was worried about me and about what his father would say after he saw the damage to the motorcycle.

When I got home, my uncle and aunt were very upset with me, but I was in pain and too tired to argue, so I closed my bedroom door and fell asleep. A little while later, my uncle knocked at my door and told me to come out and greet some visitors, who turned out to be Bandi Steiner, the son of a well-known lawyer in Levice – my mother had been his legal secretary – and Bandi's friend Joe Tomasov, whom

I had never met. Bandi and Joe had studied engineering together at Charles University in Prague. Uncle Jozko had enormous respect for Bandi, in part because he greatly admired Bandi's father.

Bandi explained that his friend would be in Levice for three weeks. Joe was single and Bandi and his wife, Susy, had promised that they would show him a good time and introduce him to a nice girl. They had both thought of me. We all talked for a while. I wasn't interested in Joe, but I was polite. When they invited me to go with them to a restaurant with dancing, I pulled up my skirt, showing them my injured thighs, and apologized that I wouldn't be able to join them. To my surprise, Uncle Jozko refused to accept my excuses and volunteered to go with us as a chaperone.

We arrived at the Denk restaurant and I danced with all of them, forgetting all about the pain in my legs. I liked dancing so much that I thought there was no life without it. We were there for quite a while. For the first time, my uncle didn't rush me home. Joe invited me to go with him to the public swimming pool the next day, but I didn't give him a definite answer. As soon as we got home, my uncle said the following words, which were to be my destiny: "Agi, this is the first boy that I can tell you your dear mother, my sister, Katka, would agree is a serious, intelligent and reliable man. You need someone like that because you are still childish."

After our talk, I was awake all night. The next day, my uncle insisted that I go to the swimming pool to meet Joe. I felt as if I had a fever, but he told me that there was no good reason for me not to go, and that I should stop thinking of Peter and his motorcycle. I was confused but went to the swimming pool anyway. I didn't recognize Joe until he came over and said hello. After that, we met every day and really enjoyed each other's company. It wasn't easy to end my relationship with Peter, but after several meetings, Joe told me that his intentions toward me were serious. He was about to immigrate to Australia – he already had a landing permit and was going to leave with Bandi Steiner and his wife, and another friend, Harry Golan, and his wife. The four of them had all finished university together in Prague. Joe told me that he was in love with me and that he would be the happiest man in the world if I would marry him and join them.

I wasn't sure what to do. I liked Joe, but not enough to travel to the other end of the world with him. He left Levice after three weeks and asked me to give his request serious thought. Bandi and Susy put pressure on me, telling me exactly the same thing as Jozko: if I refused Joe, I would always regret my decision as I would never again meet such a valuable man.

~

Joe Tomasov was born on May 25, 1920, in Trstena Orava, the fifth child of Kalman and Margita Tomaschoff (née Duschnitz).[3] The family had lived for generations in a beautiful mountainous region of north Slovakia called Orava. Joe was the fifth of six children and was two years old when his younger brother, Julius, was born. Six months later, his mother became gravely ill. She suffered from deep depression and had to be medically treated – she was hospitalized on and off from the latter part of 1922 onward. She never fully recovered and was unable to care for her children. This placed a huge burden on the whole family, as Joe's father could not take care of six children by himself.

Fortunately, Joe's extended family stepped in to help. His father took care of four of the children: the eldest, William, who was nine years old, Eugene, eight, Robert, six, and Julius, the youngest, who was by then only six months old. Kalman hired a nanny to help care for the baby and the three boys and moved the whole family to Budapest. Joe, now almost three years old, was adopted by his maternal grand-

---

3   Like Agnes's father, Joe changed his name from Tomaschoff to Tomasov in 1946 because "Tomaschoff" was German-sounding and after World War II, anti-German sentiment was very prevalent.

parents, the Duschnitz family, who lived in the Zubrohlava region of Orava. He stayed there until he was six, as soon as he was old enough to begin school, and then his father brought him to Budapest to join his four brothers. He had to start school in a new language, Hungarian, which he didn't understand at all, having grown up speaking Slovak. His only sister, Aranka, was adopted at the age of five by Kalman's brother, Florian Tomaschoff, and his wife, Sidonia, who lived in the Orava region of Slovakia and had no children of their own. Aranka was raised by them and lived with them until she married in 1942 at the age of twenty-four. Florian and Sidonia, who were extremely good-hearted people, thought of her as their own daughter.

When Joe was twelve the family was struck by tragedy again – Kalman Tomaschoff died suddenly at the age of fifty-three. The children were now left without a mother or a father. Once again Uncle Florian and Aunt Sidonia came to the rescue: they adopted both Joe and his ten-year-old brother, Julius. The eldest brother, William, who was nineteen, was old enough to work and take care of himself, and both Robert and Eugene stayed with him and finished school in Budapest. In 1933, a year after his father's death, Eugene, Joe's second eldest brother, immigrated to Palestine at the age of nineteen. That same year, Joe's uncle Florian arranged his bar mitzvah.[4] What should have been a joyous occasion was very sad for him because there were only twelve people in attendance. No mother, no father and only the two siblings who lived with him.

Joe went to high school in Dolný Kubín – it was about five kilometres from home and he had to walk there and back every day. When he graduated in 1939 he applied to the university, but by then Jews in Slovakia were no longer allowed admittance to the universities. He

---

4   A bar mitzvah is the Jewish ritual and family celebration that marks the religious coming of age of a boy at the age of thirteen. For more information, see the glossary.

found a job as an English teacher with Vera Spira's family in Nováky – the same Vera Spira that I later met through Hashomer Hatzair. Joe stayed there for several months and during that time met a very influential Jewish family named Quittner. The Quittners employed him during the critical years between 1940 and 1942, protecting him from deportation.[5]

In September 1942, Joe was sent to the Jewish labour camp in Nováky.[6] Once again, luck was on Joe's side – Dr. Spira, the camp's chief doctor, saved him from several selections that would have seen him deported to Auschwitz. In 1944, he was sent out of the labour camp to work as a bricklayer in an area surrounded by mountains into which partisans were parachuted from England and the Soviet Union. When the national Slovak uprising began in August 1944, he and twenty other Jewish inmates of the labour camp managed to escape and join the liberation army. He survived in the mountains as a partisan until the Red Army arrived in March 1945.

After liberation, Joe began searching for the survivors of his family. With the exception of Aranka, Robert and Eugene, they had all perished. William had been deported to Majdanek, Poland in 1942, along with his youngest brother, Julius. Both perished in the Majdanek death camp. Robert survived the war in Bucharest, Romania and immigrated to Israel in 1948. Aranka survived the war in the Slovak Mountains; after the war she immigrated first to Israel and then to Canada. In all, approximately twenty-seven close mem-

---

5 Between 1940 and 1942, about 3,500 Jews were sent to labour camps in Sered, Nováky and Vhyne. These camps were set up by the Slovak Jewish Center in an effort to spare Jews from deportation. In 1942, over 58,000 Slovak Jews were deported to Auschwitz and the Lublin district. For more information, see the glossary.

6 Nováky was the largest labour camp in Slovakia and was divided into two sections – one was a labour camp and the other a transit camp, where prisoners were deported to death camps in Auschwitz and Majdanek.

bers of Joe's family were tragically murdered in the concentration and death camps.

When he learned the fate of his family, Joe, at the age of twenty-five, recognized that he had to face reality and take care of himself. He decided to study civil engineering. He received a scholarship that supported him modestly and worked part-time during his studies to make ends meet. He graduated from the University of Prague as a professional civil engineer in 1949. It was at this point that he made up his mind to emigrate to Australia with his two colleagues, Bandi Steiner and Harry Golan, and their wives. He had obtained his landing permit in April 1949.

~

Three days after Joe had left Levice without my answer to his proposal, my aunt handed me a thick envelope from him. She asked me to take my cousin Katka to the park, where I could read the letter in private. Unbelievably, on my way to the park, I actually lost the unopened letter. I searched everywhere, but it was nowhere to be found. When I told my uncle, he was furious and accused me of doing it on purpose. The next day, Joe phoned and asked me for my reaction to his letter. I had to tell him that I had lost it. Joe explained over the phone what his letter had said: he wanted me to know that my decision was crucial to him because without me, his life wouldn't be the same. He also said that I needed to make a decision quickly because there were signs that the ruling Communist regime might close the borders at any time and, if they did, we would no longer be able to get out of the country.

I decided to join him. Joe sent his landing permit back to Australia and asked them to add my name to it. After long telephone conversations (which cost a fortune), I agreed to invite him to Bardejov and introduce him to my father and the rest of my family. I announced my decision to my uncle Jozko, who was delighted. He called my father to let him know that Joe and I would be arriving within the next few days. Jozko told my father that he had met Joe and fully approved of my decision. Now it was up to my father to give his blessing.

Before I left for Bardejov, my uncle had a serious talk with me about financial issues. He knew that my father was very wealthy and he didn't want my stepmother to cheat me out of what was mine. He also knew that Joe was an orphan without any means, and he didn't want us to leave for Australia penniless. He asked me, "How much of a dowry will your father give you?" I had no idea about money matters, so I told him, "I don't know, maybe 30,000 crowns," which had the value of approximately $300.00. My uncle shouted at me that I wasn't being adult and responsible. "If he gave you ten times that much, it would still be ridiculous." He couldn't understand that I just wasn't interested in anything to do with money.

A few days later, we met Joe in Bardejov. I had arrived the day before him and the whole town was already full of rumours that I was getting married. Magda's mother, Julish, asked me who the man was. I told her, "He has blue eyes, dark hair, long eyelashes and he's an engineer." She laughed and said to my father that I was still a child.

The whole family went to the railway station to wait for Joe. After talking to him for several hours, my father agreed to hold an engagement dinner for us the next week. It was a small dinner, besides the immediate family, only Radacs Manci, a friend of my father's, was invited. This was in mid-July and we decided that we would get married on August 7, 1949 at the Hotel Denk in Levice, where we had met for the first time.

After the engagement dinner Joe and I went for a walk in the park and my father lent us his valuable Leica camera to take with us. The two of us discussed my decision to go to Australia and when I thought about being parted from my father, my uncle and Ivanko, I started to cry. I told Joe that I needed more time and that he should go without me. I told him that maybe I would join him after I finished my studies in Bratislava. In the heat of our discussion, we left without my father's camera, but fortunately, Joe ran back to the park and found it.

When we confided to my father that I just couldn't imagine leaving everyone behind and moving so far away, my father – and my stepmother – told me that it was too late to change my mind. That night I wept, thinking that my father was happy to finally get rid of me. The next day, we went ahead with our wedding preparations. Joe returned to Prague and I went to stay with Aunt Lotte and Uncle Sanyi in Košice in order to have a dressmaker make a few dresses for my wedding and for the trip to Australia. The most extraordinary thing happened while I was in Košice. I was walking along the street with Aunt Lotte when we met my friend Vera Spira, from the Hashomer Hatzair summer camp, and her mother. We were excited to see each other. Vera had told me that she was going to get married right after high school, so I told her, "You must already be married, but I have a surprise for you – I'm getting married next week!" "I'm not married yet," Vera answered, "but I will be very soon. Then my new husband and I are going to move to Israel with my parents and my brother." They asked me who the lucky man was. "You wouldn't know him because he is from Orava," I told her. Mrs. Spira said that they knew lots of people from Orava, and asked, "What's his name?" When I replied, "Joe Tomasov," they just turned and walked away without any explanation. My aunt was shocked. "We have to find out more about your future husband," she declared. "This reaction from Mrs. Spira and her daughter is extremely suspicious." She decided to go to the Spiras' home to find out what was going on. I was embarrassed, but she insisted that I go with her. Dr. Spira was the chief doctor of Košice's police force so it was easy for us to find out where they lived. When we got there, though, Mrs. Spira and Vera weren't home yet.

Aunt Lotte then went straight to Dr. Spira's office and told him the whole story. Dr. Spira was very honest with us and said, "I have to tell you the truth. We've known Joe Tomaschoff since he was nineteen years old. He was in our house as an English teacher and comes from a very respectable family. Later, when I was the chief doctor of the

Nováky labour camp, I saved him several times from deportation. My wife and daughter were sure that he would marry Vera. His sister, Aranka, assured us of it. Given this, you shouldn't be surprised at their reaction. Nonetheless, I wish you good luck – you have made the right choice." I almost kissed him before I left.

After I returned to Bardejov with my new dresses and shoes, Uncle Jozko arranged our application for a civil wedding at city hall and our wedding lunch. In fact, Uncle Jozko arranged the whole wedding. My father, stepmother and my best friend, Magda, travelled to Levice. Unfortunately, Ivanko wasn't able to attend our wedding because he was in summer camp. My father and my stepmother were stopping over in Levice for my wedding on their way to Karlovy Vary Spa for a vacation. [7] When we arrived in Levice on August 6, we all stayed in the Hotel Denk. I was feeling a bit like *The Bartered Bride*. [8]

On the evening of our arrival in Levice, we all went out for a nice dinner and dancing. Joe and I decided that we would go straight to Bratislava after the wedding and spend our wedding night at the Hotel Carlton. The next day we would go to Prague, where Joe still had his student room. From there we would go to Mariánské Lázně for our honeymoon and make day trips to nearby Karlovy Vary, where I would be able to see my father and Ivanko, who was meeting his parents there after camp.

August 7, 1949, was a hot summer day. Our wedding ceremony was short, followed by an elegant lunch. We had eighteen guests, including my father, stepmother, Uncle Jozko, Aunt Ica and my cousin Katka, Uncle Sanyi and Aunt Lotte, Magda, our witnesses Bandi Steiner and his wife, Susy, Susy's parents, Mr. and Mrs. Takacs, Mrs.

---

7   Karlovy Vary, about 130 kilometres from Prague in western Bohemia, is a popular tourist destination known for its spas and mineral springs.

8   A Czech opera composed between 1863 and 1866, *The Bartered Bride* tells the story of a couple that cleverly works their way to be together, in defiance of the bride's previously arranged marriage to someone else.

Feldmann – the mother of my previous boyfriend, Gyuri – and a few others. Mrs. Feldmann couldn't stop crying through the whole wedding, lamenting that she had lost me. Joe nicknamed her "orkán," which means heavy downpour.

Musicians played lovely Gypsy music and my father sang beautiful Hungarian songs such as "Asszony lett a lányból" (The Girl Will Become the Woman). Some of the lyrics of the song translate as "A woman develops from a girl. A rose comes from a bud. Many sweet minutes will come from many happy hours, and from the many happy days come happy years. Black hair slowly becomes snow white." Uncle Jozko whispered to me, "If only your mother could be here." I answered, "She is here, beside me" and started to cry. It was very moving.

Our modest wedding eventually came to an end and everybody went their own way. Suddenly my husband and I were on our own, knowing that we had to face life together, without moral support. Joe had lost his parents, I didn't have a mother, and my father was more concerned with his wife and son.

Uncle Jozko accompanied us to the railway station, where we caught the train to Bratislava for our wedding night at the elegant Hotel Carlton. When we arrived, Joe's best friend, Erwin Slezak, was waiting for us in the hotel lobby. We spent some time talking to him and another friend, Tomy Golan, about our future. The next day we travelled to Prague to stay in Joe's student room. He introduced me to his landlady, a middle-aged woman named Mrs. David. Her first reaction to me was not flattering. "For goodness' sake," she said, "how old are you, little girl? Have you lost your mind getting married in your teenage years?" It was not an encouraging welcome. Joe told me not to take it to heart – Mrs. David had recently gotten divorced and was bitter.

The next day, we left for our ten-day honeymoon to Mariánské Lázně spa. While we were there, as planned, we visited Karlovy Vary. I was really looking forward to seeing my father and brother. When we arrived, Ivanko was running around with his friend, Laci Horak, playing in the elevators. My parents and Laci Horak's parents had always spent the holidays together in Karlovy Vary. Magda and her mother were also there.

Joe and I enjoyed our honeymoon. We went dancing and went to the theatre. But all too soon it was over and we returned to Prague for about two weeks. Joe was still very focused on immigrating to Australia. Everyone was advising us to leave Prague – which was already under Communist rule – so we moved to Slovakia where we hoped it would be easier to obtain the necessary documents for immigration because we had been married there. We decided to go to Bardejov to wait for our documents, but my stepmother refused to let us stay with my father and her for a few weeks. I was embarrassed and ashamed. She told me to go to Levice and let my uncle find us short-term living arrangements.

Having no other choice, we went on to Levice, where Uncle Jozko found us a room to sublet. We moved in and waited for our exit visas. Just before the end of October, our exit visas were refused and Joe's dream collapsed. I have to admit that I was relieved – I didn't want to leave my family – but for Joe's sake I pretended to be upset. At the beginning of November 1949 we returned to Prague, where Joe's student room was fortunately still vacant. Joe started to work as an engineer in a very prestigious company called Energoprojekt. He was very successful as a power plant design engineer. I had already lost one year of university, so I was advised to attend a preparatory program at Charles University, after which they could recommend me to a medical university for the 1950–1951 school year.

A Family of My Own

I had never visited Prague before I got married – everything I experienced there was new. The city was the cultural centre of Czechoslovakia, full of brilliant theatre and world-class concert halls. I had never encountered anything like this in Bardejov and I was looking forward to enjoying the delights of this famous metropolis.

Our married life began with some complications. We lived in one room with a bathroom that we shared with other tenants. To ensure privacy, we had to make a bathroom schedule. Joe unfortunately hadn't explained how to use the propane water heater when the hot water was on, and the first time it was my turn to take a shower, the heater burst. I ran naked out to the corridor screaming that there had been an explosion. Mr. Kybal, one of the other tenants, who was a very puritanical bachelor, saw a naked woman for the first time in his life. He was so embarrassed that he never said hello to me again during the two years that we lived there.

But all in all, we were happy. We made new friends and lived a rich, cultural life, which was easy to do in Prague. We went to some of Prague's twenty-six theatres; we attended concerts and cabarets with our new friends, the Grunfelds; and we went dancing with other friends on Saturday nights. I continued with school and by the end of June 1950, I was recommended for a place at Comenius University for the 1950–1951 school year starting in October. Joe was also achieving success at work and was promoted to a leading position in civil engineering.

At the same time, however, the political situation in Czechoslovakia under Communist rule was gradually deteriorating for Jews, especially, after 1951. It was complicated – many of the leaders of the Communist Party, such as Secretary General Rudolf Slánský, were Jewish, and many Jews in the Party were devoted to socialism in reaction to the tragedy of the Holocaust. However, the party was directed from Moscow and Joseph Stalin was an enemy of the Jews, instigating antisemitism in all the U S S R's East European satellite countries, including East Germany, Poland, Czechoslovakia, Hungary, Romania and Bulgaria.[1] Over the course of several years, Soviet show trials – kangaroo courts – prosecuted some of the most devoted Jewish members of the Party as Zionist enemies of the state, as capitalists and as sympathizers with the West. Thousands were jailed, sentenced to years of hard labour or executed. Relatives of the victims were evicted from their apartments and denied decent jobs.

As young newlyweds, though, we just tried to get on with our new life together. Not long after we were married, Joe invited some colleagues over for dinner. He knew that I didn't know how to cook, so he bought me a cookbook and we decided on a simple menu. I thought that the simplest thing to cook would be beef soup, even though it was impossible to get any fresh vegetables in Prague at that time. We bought a lot of meat and I asked my landlady if the beef soup would be okay without any vegetables in it. She gave me some of the vegetables that she had preserved by pressing them in salt. Being

------

1   Joseph Stalin, first General Secretary of the Communist Party of the Soviet Union's Central Committee from 1922 until his death in 1953, embarked on a campaign between 1948 and 1953 against elements that he believed posed a threat to his totalitarian control of Soviet society. The main targets of his campaign were prominent members of the Jewish community, writers and artists. Czech policy followed Soviet policy and embarked on a similar antisemitic campaign.

totally ignorant when it came to cooking, I put a large amount of the salty vegetables directly into the pot. After they had been cooking for two hours, I confessed to Joe that the soup was horribly salty, that it looked dark and wasn't edible. I began to cry, but Joe told me that we could neutralize the salt with sugar. We poured in a sizable amount of sugar and after that, even the meat tasted disgusting. Joe ran out to buy a cake so that we would at least have dessert.

When the guests arrived, my eyes were red from crying, but the table was set beautifully. After they had tasted the soup, they said politely, "We aren't used to tomato soup." I took the soup away and began to serve potatoes with the meat that I had removed from the pot. When they had tasted the oddly flavoured meat, our guests said, "Please don't worry about us, we aren't really hungry." Only the cake and coffee were edible. That was my debut as a cook.

By now, I was approaching twenty and had a strong desire to have a child. My husband was almost thirty, which seemed old to me. We talked about it and decided to go ahead and have a baby, even though we had no idea who would help me in sharing the responsibilities a child would bring. There was a coupon system for rationing food in Czechoslovakia at that time, and we joked about the advantages of being able to get pregnancy coupons and multiple food coupons for children, as well as regular adult coupons for Joe.

I became pregnant in June 1950, so when the time came for me to start university, I was already four months pregnant – I was due at the beginning of March 1951. I had to decide what to do with the baby while I was at school, so Joe began to look for help. We interviewed several people, but I couldn't stop thinking about how happy my mother would have been if she had been able to raise me. I felt like a terrible person for being willing to give up my child for my career and allow my child to be raised by strangers. Even though Joe disagreed with me, I decided to give up my studies and raise my baby myself. I made this decision in reaction to the pain I had experienced in my own childhood – I felt psychologically damaged.

The months passed by and I had a healthy pregnancy. I was advised not to be alone during the last few days before giving birth, so Aunt Lotte came to Prague to stay with me. My obstetrician, Dr. Bela Feher, was a good friend of ours. He wasn't married and lived in the hospital, so he was always available. Two weeks before the baby was born we had a false alarm and hurried to the hospital with my suitcase. When we arrived, however, the doorman told us that we wouldn't be having the baby that day. The doctor confirmed his diagnosis and we returned home. I was so embarrassed.

I was very glad when Aunt Lotte arrived – she had a great sense of humour and was full of life. On the evening before the baby was born, March 12, 1951, Lotte wanted to go dancing at a place called Zlatá Husa. We danced until ten o'clock, when I started having pains in my back. I told Joe and Aunt Lotte that I thought I was having the baby. We ran to the streetcar, hurried to our apartment and picked up the suitcase that was already prepared. Aunt Lotte stayed in the apartment while we called a cab. The pains were getting stronger and stronger. Joe and I arrived at the hospital Apolinářská-prvni Zemska porodnice, where fortunately Dr. Feher was on duty. He examined me and told Joe to go home since the baby wouldn't be arriving before morning. We reminded Dr. Feher that my mother had suffered a retained placenta and experienced a postpartum infection. Joe left and the nurses put me in a special room called the *hekarna*, which is Czech slang for the "yelling room." There were nine women already there and the yelling was very loud.

I had read a lot of health-related books during my pregnancy and the books all said that older women often had a harder time during childbirth than younger women. A woman was screaming loudly next to me and I asked her how long she had been in labour. "Eighteen hours and I'm in such terrible pain," she responded. I thought that she must be a much older woman since she was having such a difficult time, so I asked her how old she was. When she replied that she was eighteen, I got so scared that I called the nurse. After examining me, she said, "I'm calling Dr. Feher right away," and another nurse rolled me into the delivery room.

I was in terrible pain, but according to my health books I wasn't supposed to exhaust myself because the pains would be getting stronger, so I didn't scream. Dr. Feher arrived right away – by this time it was about one o'clock in the morning. He examined me and said, "Agi, we're going to be having this baby very soon." A very painful hour and a half later, I heard my baby cry for the first time. When Dr. Feher exclaimed, "It's a boy!" I started to cry as well and asked him to let me see my son. The doctor and nurses told me to wait until they could clean him up and make him presentable. It was now 1:30 in the morning on March 13, 1951.

From the moment I heard my baby cry, I was overcome with a deep love for him. I also felt a tremendous amount of responsibility. Despite everything I'd already been through, this was the moment when I needed my mother the most.

The nurses hadn't brought the baby back yet when Dr. Feher came into the room and told me that, unfortunately, history was repeating itself. My placenta hadn't come out in full, so he would have to perform a procedure to remove what was left in my uterus, called a dilation and curettage (D and C). He explained that he couldn't give me general anesthesia because I was going to be breastfeeding and it might be dangerous for the baby. He could only give me laughing gas to lessen the pain. I hadn't raised my voice during delivery, but during this procedure I screamed at the top of my lungs. When it was over, I was in intense pain and had a fever. The nurses finally brought my baby to me though, which calmed me down. I thought that he was the most beautiful creature in the whole world. When they placed him beside me, I uncovered him and counted all his fingers. After too short a time, one of the nurses came in and told me that she was taking the baby to the nursery so that I could get some sleep. "You've been through a lot," she said. I begged her not to take the baby but she refused. I was so upset that I couldn't sleep.

Joe came to the hospital the next morning and was thrilled to see his son for the first time. We decided to name him Tomas. I was transferred to a room with nine other mothers and the babies were placed in a separate nursery behind a glass window. We could hear all of them crying. The hospital had a rule that the babies had to be kept away from their mothers for twenty-four hours – it was torture not being with him. My temperature was elevated and the day seemed endless. Aunt Lotte came to visit me, but all I wanted was my baby.

At about ten o'clock that night I had a vision of my baby crying. I jumped out of bed and walked on the stone floor to his room to make sure that he was all right. The nurse caught me and explained sternly that I wasn't permitted to get out of bed after a D and C. My fever persisted through the night and the next morning Dr. Feher told me that he was very disappointed in me, complaining to Joe that getting out of bed was a very childish and dangerous thing to do.

I was sharing a room with a kind woman named Mrs. Sobel, whose husband was a lawyer. She was forty years old and just three days before had lost her own baby after five months of pregnancy. It was her fourth miscarriage and she was desperate to hold Tom. Dr. Feher assured her that everything would be fine the next time as long as she remained in hospital for the full nine months of her pregnancy. Compared to her, I felt very fortunate.

Nine days after Tom was born, Dr. Feher decided to let me go home. Aunt Lotte had had to go back to Košice, but my father had come from Bardejov to stay with us. Joe and my father came to pick me up from the hospital. We packed up everything and were so distracted as we said goodbye to everybody that a nurse had to call after us, "Don't be in such a rush – you forgot your baby!"

My temperature remained elevated for six weeks and Dr. Feher came to visit me almost every second day. As soon as we got home with the baby, I began to feel anxious – Tomas had to be changed and I didn't know how. My father told me not to worry, that he had changed me when I was a baby, but the truth is that he had completely forgotten how to do it. I was also terrified of picking Tomas up because my father told me that their maid had dropped his youngest brother while giving him a bath and broken his backbone. He only lived to the age of eighteen and spent his whole life bedridden and motionless.

Tomas cried. I cried. When Joe came home from work a nurse arrived to show him how to give Tomas a bath. I was so afraid that she would drop him that I had to keep my eyes closed. Joe had to give the baby his bath every day for five months – I was too scared to do it. I worried about Tomas's health constantly. I was never satisfied with an ordinary pediatrician whose services were free of charge – I had to take Tomas to a famous, expensive professor of pediatrics, Dr. Epstein. During one visit, I complained to Dr. Epstein that Tomas had a nervous disposition. He asked me to tell him what the signs of this were. After my explanation, the professor wrote me a prescription that read, "Dear mother: These pills are to be taken twice a day, not by your baby but by you. Your baby is completely healthy, but you have to calm your nerves." The prescription was for an anti-anxiety medication.

When Tom was three months old, my girlfriend Magda was dating a famous cardiologist, Dr. Tibor Zemplenyi. I never wanted to leave Tom for a single moment, but they had invited me to join them at the Vinohradske Theatre, where the famous live performance of *Dívka s bílými vlasy* (The White-Haired Girl) was playing.[2] The theatre was only ten minutes walking distance from our home and Joe wanted me to go, so he offered to stay home with Tom. After fifteen minutes at the theatre, however, I started to get restless. In spite of Joe's promise that he would be extremely careful with Tom, I got increasingly worried. The theatre performance was excellent, but my maternal worries were stronger. I left the theatre and went home alone. Magda and

---

2 Based on the popular Chinese opera, ballet and film *Bái Máo Nǚ* by Yan Jinxuan.

Tibor were very disappointed and said that my behaviour was abnormal. Today I would agree with them. Still, my behaviour is not all that surprising for someone who had lost her mother at such a young age.

I continued to worry about Tom. I worried about his nourishment because he was such a poor eater. I turned to yet another pediatric specialist, Professor Dr. Schwejcar, who assured me that no child would die of hunger if he was drinking milk. I calmed down a little, but by Tom's first birthday, I was so exhausted that my thick hair began to fall out. I have a photo from his birthday in which I am partially bald. The three of us continued to live in one room in the apartment at Prague XII-U Riegrovych Sadu, sharing a bathroom and the kitchen, until Tom was thirteen months. It was in the nicest part of Prague, Vinohrady, which was close to a beautiful park that I visited often. I walked with the carriage every day for at least three hours no matter the weather. This is what the pediatric books recommended and I took it very seriously.

Sometime in 1952, I visited Mrs. Sobel, the woman I had met when Tom was born. She was in the hospital, where, following Dr. Feher's advice, she had stayed for the duration of her pregnancy. Miraculously, she gave birth to a beautiful baby girl. When the baby was seven weeks old, we all went to visit the Sobels; they were glowing, so thrilled to finally have a child. They were so careful with her that we had to wear masks during our visit.

When Tomas was eighteen months, we went by train to visit a friend who lived in Zbraslav, a district in the south end of Prague on the Vltava River. Tom was almost toilet-trained by then, so I didn't take any diapers with me. Because of a polio scare, we were travelling in the first-class compartment – it was less populated so we thought that there would be less risk for Tomas – and the upholstery was made of delicate material. When the conductor came to punch our tickets, he saw that Tom had unfortunately peed on the seat. The conductor threatened to punch his "pipi" if he ever did that again. From that moment on he was completely toilet-trained.

We desperately wanted to have our own apartment by then and an opportunity arose for us to move into a very small place on the periphery of Prague, in the Dejvice district, just two kilometres from the city centre. The whole unit – on the fourth floor of a building with no elevator – was only about twenty square metres, but with a terrace of almost twenty-eight square metres. Tom's second address in Prague was Ve Struhach No.18, Dejvice. It wasn't easy for us to carry the stroller up the stairs, but we were young and grateful for what we had. I often referred to our stroller as my Cadillac.

We had lived in the new place for about thirteen months when I found out that I was pregnant again. Joe and I were both overjoyed – I wanted to have a second child within three years of my first so I considered myself very blessed. However, there wasn't any place in our tiny apartment to put a second bed for the new baby. By chance we found a two-bedroom apartment on the ground floor of a building across the street that belonged to a widower. So Tom's third address was Šestidomí 6, Dejvice.

Soon after moving in we realized that our new apartment was extremely cold because it faced north and was right above the cellar. Tom began having health problems – he got recurring bouts of tonsillitis – and our visits to Dr. Epstein became so frequent that when we saw new furniture in Dr. Epstein's waiting room, Joe commented that he must have bought it with our money. During a subsequent housecall, Dr. Epstein told us that the cause of Tom's chronic tonsillitis was the cold stone floors, but, although we kept looking, we couldn't find another apartment.

There was a playground in the backyard of our apartment building and I was able to watch Tom playing from our kitchen window. I made a lot of friends through Tom's friends. I remember a particularly funny story about his friend Libuska, who was two and a half. Tom came knocking on our door crying one day, demanding to be changed right away because his pants were wet. When I told him that he should be ashamed of himself, he replied, "I didn't do it. Libuska peed into my pants."

I still felt anxious about Tom's reluctance to eat. When our neighbour Mrs. Studnicka mentioned that he loved to eat at her house with her three boys, I was overjoyed. But a few months later, a very unpleasant thing happened. Tom contracted a case of infectious jaundice from them. The whole Studnicka family had to be taken to the hospital and five days later, Tom was also admitted. All the weight he had gained from eating at her house was lost while he was sick.

One day in early February 1954, when I was about seven months pregnant and Tom was not quite three, I got a shocking telephone call. I had a cousin, Lyda Sorban, who lived in Prague with her husband and son, Yayo (Jozef), who was two years older than Tom. We used to visit each other fairly often. On this particular day, the person on the other end of the telephone told me that she was my cousin's neighbour and Lyda had asked her to call us. Yayo's parents had been handcuffed and taken away by the police and the little boy was alone, crying in the corridor of his apartment building. I asked the woman to take Yayo into her apartment until I could notify my husband. I told her not to worry, that my husband would be there as soon as possible. I hung up and called Joe – he left his office right away. When he arrived at Lyda's neighbour's apartment, he found the terrified child holding a bag of his belongings. Joe, of course, brought him straight home on the streetcar. When Yayo arrived, I embraced him and tried to reassure him that our home would be his new home and Tom would be his younger brother.

Within a few days, Yayo began to relax. He was an extremely easygoing child and was a very good influence on Tom. We had no idea where his parents had been taken or even what they had been charged with. We tried to ask Yayo's grandmother – she lived about five hundred kilometres away in Žilina – about their whereabouts, but she didn't want to get involved. She lived with her daughter, Bozenka, and worked for the Communist Party, so she was afraid of losing her job. During the almost three months that Yayo was with us, she didn't visit him once.

Time went by quickly and the next thing we knew it was April and I was due to give birth the next week. At lunchtime one day, while the boys were eating, we were disturbed by a loud knocking at our door. When I opened the door, three plainclothed policemen came into our apartment and accused me of unlawfully holding a boy by the name of Yayo Sorban. They demanded that I hand him over to them immediately. I was young and fearless, so I shouted back at them, "You are acting like the Nazis!" I tried to convince them to let me keep Yayo, but they refused. I wasn't immediate family, they said, and Yayo's parents had lost all their civil rights, so any arrangements they may have made were not legally valid. I advised them that Yayo had a grandmother in Žilina, but when I called her she refused to take him.

By this time Joe had come home from work. He also pleaded with the officers not to take Yayo away but nothing we said had any effect – they had a court order to take Yayo into government care. Yayo hid in a clothes closet. I can still hear the heartrending sound as he whimpered, "You told me you loved me, that I'm a good boy. Don't let them take me." We told him that he would only be gone for a few days and that he would come back to us. Unfortunately, we never were able to find out where the authorities had taken him. We felt totally dispirited and helpless. This was our first real experience with the cruelty of the Communist system in the 1950s. A few years later, we found out that Yayo had been kept in a government orphanage for a year until his mother was released from prison and they were reunited. His father remained incarcerated for another two years – both had been charged with being Zionists. The family immigrated to Israel in 1965.

A few days after this horrifying experience, on April 13, my stepmother arrived to be with Tom while I was in the hospital giving birth. I was hoping that the baby would arrive the next day, so I did everything I could think of – moving furniture and taking hot baths – to bring on labour. Joe came home around three in the afternoon and found me exhausted from moving the furniture. It was a beautiful day, so we went out for a walk with Tom and my stepmother and did some grocery shopping. We got home around seven and had just had a nice dinner when I suddenly began to cramp. Joe called Dr. Feher and asked him what we should do. He advised us to get to the hospital quickly because my first baby had come early. We kissed Tom good night, told my stepmother that we would probably be back within two hours and went to the hospital by streetcar, stopping over at Wenceslas Square for a huge milkshake.[3]

By the time we got to the hospital, it was about nine in the evening. Dr. Feher invited us in to his living quarters for a coffee. He was telling us some good jokes when, around ten, I began feeling restless. I told him that I had had a big milkshake and that's what was causing my cramps. After an examination, though, he decided that I should be admitted. Joe and Dr. Feher wished me good night and said that they would see me in the morning. Dr. Feher wasn't on duty that night, but he let the nurses know that they could find him in his room if they needed him. The nurses took me into the "yelling" room.

By eleven that night I was making frequent trips to the bathroom, cursing the milkshake. A couple of nurses observed my erratic behaviour and decided to examine me. When I climbed onto the examination table they exclaimed, "The baby's coming!" They moved quickly to help deliver the baby safely and a few minutes later I heard her cry. She was a beautiful little girl.

Dr. Feher arrived just after the baby was born and couldn't believe his eyes. He called Joe, who arrived at the hospital shortly thereafter. Joe thought at first that Dr. Feher was joking about the baby having arrived so quickly. But there she was – Katka, named after my mother, was born at 11:30 at night on April 13, 1954, just half an hour before she was due. I was the happiest woman in the world – I had a

---

3 Wenceslas Square is a main city square in Prague that is lined with shops and hotels and also serves as a hub for public gatherings, celebrations and demonstrations.

little girl I could name after my beloved mother. I had been worried that Joe and I would have a hard time conceiving a girl because there were twenty-seven boys in his family and only three girls. When they cleaned Katka up and presented her to me, I was so thrilled – she was the most beautiful baby I had ever seen. She had long black hair that they styled for her and Dr. Feher congratulated me, saying, "Agi, I'm not exaggerating. We haven't seen such a beautiful baby in a long, long time." The nurses were passing her from arm to arm. Unfortunately, I had the same problems with the placenta that I had had with Tom, but that was the only pain I experienced during Katka's birth.

I was discharged from the hospital after a week – it had been a long and difficult seven days for Joe since he didn't get along with my stepmother. To this day, Tom remembers that when we arrived home with Katka, he was sitting on the toilet. He was disappointed because he had wanted a brother and felt that we had let him down. A nurse came to our apartment to give Katka her first bath and as Tom watched her, he suddenly began to insist that the nurse take Katka back to the hospital because she was damaged. He became completely hysterical. We soon realized what was going on. Shortly before Katka was born, we had told Tom an amusing story from his own childhood: he frequently played with his private parts and I had consulted our pediatrician to ask what to do about it. The doctor's advice was to discourage the activity by dressing him in tight pants. "If you continue to do this," he warned Tom, "your private parts will fall off and you'll have to pee through your nose." When Tom saw baby Katka in her bath, he was horrified, "She must have played with her private part," he wailed, "because it's already fallen off. She'll have to pee through her nose from now on!" We tried to calm him down, but he just kept on crying and repeating those same words.

The story didn't end there. The first time that I took Katka out for a walk in her carriage the neighbours I met in the backyard congratulated me but added, "Such a pity that this beautiful girl is so handicapped." I asked them what on earth they were talking about. My neighbours explained that Tom had complained to everybody that our new baby had no private parts and wouldn't be able to pee. Since it was a beautiful spring day near the end of April, I undressed my new daughter in front of them so they could see that my Katka was a perfectly healthy, happy baby girl. She was eating well, which was a huge relief since I had worried so much about Tom, and she also had a calm temperament. We went to Bardejov on vacation that summer and my stepmother couldn't help commenting, "How could such a nervous person as you have such a calm, happy child?"

Near the end of May, when Katka was six weeks old, Joe was sent to Hungary on a business trip. I didn't want to stay alone with the children, so Aunt Ica and cousin Katka, who was now seven years old, came from Levice to visit. Aunt Ica soon started to complain that she wasn't getting a chance to enjoy all the entertainment Prague had to offer, so one Saturday evening our neighbour Mrs. Lafkova offered to babysit all three children. In return, she asked me to save all the leftovers from Katka's bottles to feed to her chickens. Because Katka was such a good eater, however, it took me two or three days to collect one full bottle of leftover milk.

Aunt Ica and I went to a well-known restaurant called Vltava, where a famous singer named Rudolf Cortés was performing. To our amazement, he came to our table during the dance program to ask my aunt if he could dance with me. I was not yet twenty-four years old and not bad looking – my aunt and I were both very flattered. We had a very successful evening and went back home by streetcar.

When we arrived home, we went straight to bed. I was almost asleep when Katka's crying woke me up. I automatically went to the kitchen and took her bottle out of the refrigerator. I mistakenly warmed up water instead of fresh milk, so I warmed up another bottle and tried to feed Katka. I couldn't understand why she was eating so slowly until I realized that I was feeding her from the leftover bottle, the one meant for the chickens. I got extremely upset because I knew that many children were dying of diarrhea. I called an ambulance and they took Katka and me to the Children's Hospital. After we arrived in the emergency ward, I shouted, "Quick! Clean out her stomach! I poisoned her!"

The hospital staff pumped out her stomach and not long after brought her out to me. My beautiful little girl looked like an old woman. She was exhausted and immediately fell asleep. The staff sent me home and advised me to keep a close eye on her for twenty-four hours. Luckily, Katka was fine. The next day our pediatrician told me that I had overreacted and that the entire procedure had been unnecessary. After sleeping for two hours, Katka woke up hungry and ate normally. She smiled as if nothing had happened and we thanked God that everything was okay. Joe returned from his business trip and Uncle Jozko came to pick up his family a few days later. My aunt told them the whole embarrassing story.

On Katka's first birthday, the child who was always smiling and easygoing became unhappy when the photographer arrived. She stayed in a bad mood, wouldn't smile and kept her hand on her ear. After the photographer left, I decided that she must have an ear infection. We went to the Children's Hospital right away, where they confirmed my diagnosis. This was our second warning to move from our cold apartment. After a few weeks, we found an apartment downtown – Tom and Katka's new address was Prague I-Havelská 9. The apartment was just a five-minute walk from Wenceslas Square and the Old Town Square, the location of a major tourist attraction called the Orloj, the famous old town clock. The clock was especially meaningful to us – Tom would only eat when the clock's apostle figurines appeared every hour on the hour, so I spent lots of time there feeding him. It was a paradox that Katka, who was thirteen months old, ate solid food while I still had to grind all of Tom's food. The result was that Katka weighed the same as her four-year-old brother. Our neighbour and occasional babysitter Mrs. Lafkova called Katka *parádní číslo,* which means "beautiful one." In spite of all the minor difficulties we went through, Joe and I felt blessed by our two beautiful children.

In the Hands of the Secret Police

During the summer of 1955, I took both children on a holiday with Mrs. Lafkova to Bardejovské Spa on the outskirts of Bardejov. Once again, my stepmother had refused to let us stay in my father's home. Joe had had to stay behind in Prague, but planned on joining us for the last two weeks of our holiday.

While I was there, Uncle Jozko came to visit for a few days along with another man, Berti Knapp, a relative on my mother's side from Vienna. When Joe came to meet us in Bardejov, my immediate instinct was to tell him that we should cut off all ties with Berti. I was afraid that any connection with him would bring tragedy to our family. The Communist regime in Czechoslovakia – like those in other countries in the Soviet sphere – was highly suspicious of all visitors from the capitalist West – such as Vienna – and I was afraid that they would turn their suspicions on us for encouraging this "subversive" contact. Joe, however, was very naïve about the political dangers all around us and didn't believe in women's intuition. When I asked my father to talk to him, Joe became extremely angry, but I told him that I was afraid that we would end up being the *gepore-hindl* (sacrificial lambs) while Berti Knapp remained free to enjoy his life in Vienna.

As it turned out, I was right – we were on the brink of a new catastrophe. On December 16, 1955, Joe arrived home from work earlier than usual. He told me that a car would be arriving shortly to drive him to the power plant in Hodonín, almost three hundred kilometres away, where he was the chief engineer. I was not happy that I would have to take care of both children alone while he was gone, especially since Tom was still recuperating from a bout of whooping cough.

The winter days were getting really short, so I put the children to bed early and began to read my book, *The American Tragedy* by Theodore Dreiser. I asked Joe not to wake me up if I fell asleep and to close the door quietly when he left. Not long after, I heard an insistent knocking at the door accompanied by loud voices. I rushed out of the bedroom where we slept with both children and saw seven men restraining Joe. I was terrified, but roared at them to get out of our home right away or I would call the police. "Calm down," one of the men declared. "We're from the StB (state police) and we're taking your husband in for questioning. We'll bring him back when we're finished with him."[1] I will never forget that moment, seeing Joe with his hands up, being taken away by two of those men. We didn't even have a chance to say goodbye.

The other five men stayed in our apartment. By this time I was more angry than scared and shouted, "Go away and don't wake up my children." I didn't understand what was going on. They began a thorough search of our apartment, which of course, woke up the children. I took Katka in my arms as they looked under her mattress for guns. Tom started having a coughing attack. I continued to threaten the men but they just disregarded me. They took all the cash that I had in the apartment and every document they could find, including the children's bankbooks for the accounts that my father had opened for them when they were born. After I had managed to calm the children down, I found the police searching the kitchen.

---

1   The StB (in Czech, Státní bezpečnost) was the secret police organization that investigated suspected anti-Communist activity in Czechoslovakia. They used intimidation and fear to force confessions from supposed "traitors" and also relied on civilian informants.

At that point, I recognized one of them. He was from Bardejov and was one of about twenty students who had been expelled from high school when I was there for involvement in an underground Catholic fascist organization that was agitating against the existing regime.[2] I said to him, "You know who I am and I know who you are. I will tell people about your past." He looked frightened and called me by my first name, telling me that he would help me. They continued to search our apartment until almost midnight. Another one of the men also pretended to be nice – he told me his name and said, "If your husband isn't back by tomorrow and you have any questions, you can find me at the StB headquarters at Bartolomějská 4." I asked why they were searching our home, but they didn't answer. I thought that it might be connected to some problem at the Hodonín power plant. Before they left, they warned me not to tell anyone about their visit, not even my father.

I couldn't sleep all that night; I felt that our dream life was coming to an end. I was twenty-five years old, helpless and alone in a big city with two small children. In the morning, when I woke Tom and Katka, they came into my bed and Tom asked where his father was. I was filled with fear, anxious that I couldn't tell anybody what had happened. I didn't even have money to buy milk and bread for the next day. I had no idea what else to do, so I fed the children, dressed them and headed to the StB headquarters.

I reported to the security guard and asked for the person who had given me his name and pretended to be nice to me during the search. He told me to wait on the other, sunnier side of the street with my kids. It was mid-December and quite cold. Tom was less than five years old, yet very smart for his age. He said to the security

---

2 The Catholic fascist movement in Slovakia was both antisemitic and anti-Communist. After the war, both when the Slovak Democratic Party held a majority in the Slovak National Council and under the Communists, Catholic groups were prohibited from formally organizing.

guard, "Do you know why the sun doesn't shine here? It's because God doesn't like you because you took my dad." I hadn't even realized that he had been listening to my explanation of why I was there. I got flustered but the guard said, "Don't worry, young lady. I have kids too." I calmed down a bit and went to wait on the other side of the street.

After about half an hour, the guard called us in to speak to the officer. His manner to me was now very cold as he explained that my husband had committed a crime against the state and that I should be grateful that I wasn't involved. Both horrified and terrified, I began to yell at him that he was the same man who had taken all my money and forbidden me to contact my own father. I repeated that he was acting like a Nazi. How would I feed my children? I asked. At that point the officer opened his file and gave me back some of the money that he had taken from my apartment. He also told me that I was now free to contact my father in Bardejov and my uncle in Levice. He advised me to go to Joe's office to pick up his remaining salary. I asked him whether I could see my husband, sensing that Joe was very close. To that request he responded brutally, "Leave immediately before I have you arrested." I was disgusted. I took the money and left with the children. Just before I reached the door, he ominously added that this wasn't the end of our discussion – he would be investigating me as well.

The children and I went home – I felt somewhat better knowing that I had permission to contact my father and uncle, even though I had watched the StB men put wiretaps on my phone the night before. When I finally got in touch with my father and uncle after several attempts, I said only, "Come over immediately, I'm very sick." That same day, I went to Joe's office to see his boss, Mr. Ing Dolidze, the chief engineer. He was an extremely kind elderly man who was originally from Russia. To my amazement, he knew what had happened and told me not to worry – he needed Joe's expertise and he wasn't about to stand by and watch those gangsters destroy his best engineer.

He assured me that we would stay in touch and arranged for me to have what we were owed from Joe's salary. "Come back in three days and we'll update each other," he said. He promised me that he and the company would fight for Joe's release. He didn't make any attempt to hide the fact that he was against the Communist regime.

My father and uncle arrived exhausted and worried, expecting me to be very sick; Uncle Jozko had been afraid that I would die at the same age as my mother. I explained what had happened and why I couldn't tell them anything over the telephone. They seemed relieved that at least I wasn't ill.

Later that evening, the StB showed up at my door again, telling me that this time they needed to take me for questioning. They said that I would be back in two hours. We left the house at six o'clock on a dark, December night. I wasn't afraid at all during the interrogation. Whenever they raised their voices, I raised mine. When they began focusing their questions on connections to Zionism, I told them again that the Communist regime was no better than the Nazis. They threatened me with jail, telling me that my children would be taken away from me. I was so mixed up by what was happening that for a moment I actually preferred the thought of jail to coping alone with the insanity around me.

Before I left the interrogation room, the officers told me that I would have to go to work in a factory, as wives of political prisoners did not deserve anything better. Joe had never been a member of the Communist Party, which made him suspect from the beginning, but I still didn't know why they had arrested him.

It was almost midnight when I left the police station. I arrived home to find my father and uncle in the midst of an argument because they assumed that I had been arrested – I was only supposed to be gone for two hours but had been gone for just over six hours. They had been arguing about who would take which child.

The next day I went to see Mr. Dolidze again and let him know what the StB were forcing me to do. It was a few days before Christmas

– in Communist Czechoslovakia Christmas wasn't an official celebration, but there were a few days of holiday around New Year's Day. Mr. Dolidze assured me that he would find me a job in an office in the new year. He also told me that all the employees of Energoprojekt, a very prestigious design institute, had signed a petition for Joe's release and it had been sent to the Ministry of the Interior. As I was leaving, he handed me an envelope with a substantial amount of money for Christmas. I expressed my deepest gratitude toward this extraordinary man and all of Joe's colleagues. Their support lifted my spirits during this difficult time.

A few days after Joe's arrest, Mrs. Sobel, whom I had met in the pregnancy ward, showed up at our apartment with her three-year-old daughter. When she saw my state of desperation, she encouraged me to cheer up. "Get dressed and go for a walk in the park with me," she said. I hesitated, but she insisted. When we stopped to sit on a bench in the park, she confided that she knew Joe had been arrested. "There are many, many Jewish women whose husbands have been arrested," she said. "My own husband has been in jail for seven months now. What I came to tell you is that there are Jewish organizations that have funds to support us." She explained that I would receive monthly financial support that would be delivered to me in person, adding that I must keep this information in the strictest confidence – nobody was to find out. I thanked her but said that I didn't need this kind of help. "I will be getting financial support from my father," I told her. "Give it to somebody who needs the help more than me." Mrs. Sobel let me know that she was very disappointed in my response and left – she felt that, as Jews, we should all try to stick together and she just didn't understand why I wouldn't accept her help. I didn't hear from her after that.

～

After my visit to Mr. Dolidze just before Christmas 1955, I realized that I had to find some kind of daycare for twenty-month-old Katka while I was at work. Tom was being sent to Kynzwart, a government-sponsored spa where children were sent to recover from whooping cough. He was to start his eight-week treatment at the beginning of January. My father babysat the children while I went with Uncle Jozko to the daycare centre that had been suggested by the StB.

I will never forget that horrible facility. There was a long corridor and we looked into the rooms through windows; there were eighteen cribs to a room, each one holding a child dressed in a striped uniform. The children appeared clean, but seemed neglected. There were only three nurses, also in striped uniforms, who ran from crib to crib. I began to cry and ask my mother desperately for help. My uncle was shocked as well by the environment, but he tried to get me to stop crying. He didn't want to leave Katka in that place either and offered to take her to his home in Levice until my situation could be resolved. I kissed him and we left without even going into the daycare office.

When we got home, Uncle Jozko called his wife, who, fortunately, wasn't employed at that time. She was staying home to look after their eight-year-old daughter – my cousin Katka – and readily agreed to let my daughter live with them. Packing Katka's little things was heartbreaking. We all went to the railway station and I kissed her goodbye. She was crying – she just couldn't understand why I was giving her away. I consoled myself with the thought that at least I wasn't leaving her in that brutal daycare facility.

My father left the next day and that same night I suffered a terrible gall bladder attack. I called the hospital's emergency ward and a doctor came to give me a shot of morphine. He told me to go to my doctor's office the next day for a checkup. Tom was still at home with me, so I called my friend Magda for help. Her husband answered and when I explained my whole situation to him, he unpleasantly replied, "Don't call us anymore. I don't want to get in trouble." I felt so alone. Despite her husband's attitude, however, Magda arrived, apologizing for his behaviour. She stayed with Tom so that I could go to my doctor's appointment. During this difficult time in my life, I really learned who my real friends were. The gallbladder attack had made me afraid to stay alone with Tom at night. I asked another friend, Eliska Grunfeld, to stay overnight with me, which she agreed to do for me even though her young daughter, Margitka, was in a brace because of a hip dislocation. She didn't hesitate to help me, for which I will always be grateful.

I missed Katka so much; I felt wretched and stressed, and as a result, my gallbladder attacks became more frequent. I started to lose weight and thought things couldn't get any worse. I was mistaken.

Between Christmas and New Year's Day, I went to see Mr. Dolidze, who announced that he had found me a job as an assistant accountant with a company called Zasklivaci služba hlavního města Prahy (Prague Glazing Services). I told Mr. Dolidze that I didn't know anything about accounting, but he told me to take the job anyway, otherwise the authorities would force me to take a menial job. He also advised me not to tell anyone at my new place of employment that my husband had been arrested. If anyone asked, I was to say that we were separated.

I was supposed to report to the company's Communist political secretary on January 3, 1956, and tell him that Ing Dolidze had recommended me for the job. That same day, Tom left to receive treatment for his whooping cough. I asked Mr. Dolidze to arrange the start of my work at noon instead of early morning so I could take Tom to the railway station. Lots of the children at the station were crying, including Tom. I cried with him, promising that his father and I would be reunited with him soon. As soon as the train left, I rushed to my future job, where I had to fill out all kinds of paperwork.

At my new office, I reported to the political secretary, who was kind to me. He had been the caretaker in Mr. Dolidze's building before the Communists took over.[3] He introduced me to the chief ac-

---

3   After the Communist takeover, all economic sectors were nationalized and the Party functioned on some level of control at each workplace. The new regime

countant and the seven other people who worked in the same room. "This is Comrade Agnes," he told everyone, "and she will be working as an assistant to the chief accountant." My co-workers weren't very welcoming.

I worked beside the chief accountant. He piled up a lot of papers on my desk and said, "Because you have experience, you know what to do. You'll find a calculator and typewriter on your table. Do your job." He didn't explain anything to me. I was hesitant to use the adding machine because it made a loud noise whenever I touched it. After an hour of looking at the documents my boss had given me, my nerves collapsed and I started to cry. I turned to the chief accountant and said, "I have to tell you the truth. I've never worked as an accountant. My husband is in jail and I have two little children so I have to work."

My boss jumped up and embraced me. "You darling girl, why didn't you tell me right away that you are not a Communist? Why did that Communist pig, the political secretary, introduce you to us? How do you know him? Don't worry. In this room there are just friends, admirers of Jan Masaryk."[4] I explained my whole situation, starting with Mr. Dolidze and ending with my meeting with the caretaker-turned-political secretary. He shook my hand and declared, "Agnes, I am Vasek and I am going to teach you accounting. I guarantee you that within six weeks you will be my best assistant." It was bewildering to learn that in a company in the middle of a strong Communist

---

often replaced non-Communist employees with those that had proven their allegiance to Communism and devoted working-class party members were promoted to professional positions to ensure complete immersion in Communist practice and ideology.

4 Jan Masaryk was the son of Tomas Masaryk, founder and first president of Czechoslovakia. During World War II, Jan Masaryk served as foreign minister to the Czech government-in-exile, a position he retained in the provisional, Communist-dominated government established in 1945. Following the 1948 Communist coup, Masaryk died suspiciously – in 2002 it was finally determined that he had been murdered. For more information, see the glossary.

regime there were people who were secretly against Communism.

From that day on, Vasek spent every evening teaching me how to do my job and how to become proficient in accounting. He was not only a good teacher but also a good psychologist. Whenever I wasn't able to absorb everything he taught me, he encouraged me by saying, "You're a clever girl and you're progressing faster than I thought you would." Despite his kind words, however, I often felt stupid. Nonetheless, miraculously, after six weeks, I began to notice that I was becoming helpful to him. Up to that point, he had been doing all the work himself.

I found a way to repay Vasek for his kindness. He suffered from asthma and often became quite ill. His wife would come to the office in the evenings when he was teaching me and on one of her visits she told me that they wished they knew somebody in the United States who could send them the medicine that Vasek needed to get better. I suggested that if she could get the name of the medication, I would ask my sister-in-law in Canada if she could send it. I got in touch with Joe's sister, Aranka, and arranged for the medicine to be sent to Vasek. Everything went smoothly, it arrived safely within a few days.

The political situation within the company was unbelievably ironic. Once a week, during working hours, we were required to attend a political indoctrination session that was supposed to instil in us the communist ideals of Marx, Lenin and Stalin. Instead, we heard lectures on Masaryk's philosophy under the pretense that we were listening to texts from Lenin. The Communist leaders of the company, who had all previously been labourers, were uneducated and had no idea that they were listening not to Lenin's ideals but Masaryk's. Only those of us around Vasek recognized the actual content of these lectures. I was grateful for this unusual experience.

I was now working full-time, six days a week, and in the evenings Vasek was teaching me accounting until very late. By the time I got home every night I was exhausted and very lonely. My life felt miserable and empty without my children and my husband. I still didn't know where Joe was being held and I was so desperate to see Katka that I asked Vasek for some time off at the end of February. He gave me two days off in addition to Sunday, my regular day off. I took a train to Levice to spend three days with my beautiful little girl.

When I arrived at Uncle Jozko and Aunt Ica's house, Katka was playing in her crib. Her big blue eyes looked up at me, but she didn't recognize me at all. She was very attached to Uncle Jozko. He said to her, "Katka, this is your Mami." It was heartbreaking. My little girl answered, "Don't cry, Auntie Mami." The next day, Katka let me feed her, but I could tell that she didn't know that I was her mother. She was only twenty-two months old – at that age two months is a very long time.

The next two days passed very quickly and then it was time for me to return to work in Prague. I cried the whole way back on the train. I didn't know what our future held. A few days after my return from Levice, however, I received notification from the district court that my husband's trial would be held on March 12, 1956. I immediately called my father and asked him to attend the trial with me. He had exceptional local connections and could bring documents with him to impress the court.

My father arrived two days before the trial. We made an appointment with the designated judge, Dr. Kobza, who had previously been a railway mechanic. This was not unusual – in their desire to sweep away the former power structure, the Communist regime created new judges and prosecutors by appointing laymen who had had only a few months of training. When we arrived at the office of Dr. Kobza, my father presented his credentials and said, "Comrade Kobza, I find myself in a desperate situation with my daughter. She is alone in Prague and has suffered numerous gall bladder attacks, losing a tremendous amount of weight. I would like to know the outcome of tomorrow's trial so I can decide what to do with her and the grand-children." Kobza kindly replied, "Comrade Gonda, I have a daughter of the same age, so I know what you are going through. I'm happy to tell you that your son-in-law will be going home tomorrow, but he has to be more careful in the future." We were so overjoyed that we embraced him and said, "We'll see you tomorrow in court."

On our way home my father and I actually argued about what meal to prepare for Joe. I wanted to prepare a chicken stew, but my father argued that after months of near-starvation, such rich food would make him ill. I agreed to prepare a light dinner after the trial.

After a sleepless night, we arrived at the courthouse at eight o'clock the next morning. Unbeknownst to us, another person by the name of Mr. Blau was to be tried together with Joe. His wife introduced herself and sat with us in the hallway. Mrs. Blau was a few years older than me and appeared to be more relaxed than we were. She also wasn't Jewish and she and her husband didn't have any children.

I saw Joe just before the trial started. He was in handcuffs, unshaven, skinny and pale. It was awful to see him that way. I didn't see Mr. Blau but his wife told me that he was also in terrible shape.

At nine o'clock sharp the court officers let us into the room where the actual proceedings would be held. The prosecutor, Dr. Siegel, read out the accusations against Joe that were complete fabrication – I discovered that he had been arrested because he was Jewish and for the "crime" of supposedly being a "Zionist." He was also tainted in the eyes of the Communist government for having applied to immigrate to Australia in April 1949, just over a year after the February 1948 Communist revolution. After hearing all this my nerves gave out and I shouted, "Those are outright lies!" My father tried to calm me down but it didn't help. After the third warning, I was kicked out of the courtroom and had to wait outside in the corridor while my father stayed to witness the proceedings.

After about three hours, I was called in for the proclamation of the verdict. What I heard sent me into complete shock. Instead of coming home, as the presiding judge had promised the day before, Joe was sentenced to eight years in prison. I shouted at the tribunal, "This is a kangaroo court full of lies!" My father was worried that I too would be incarcerated. I called out to Joe to appeal the sentence, which he did immediately, and it was accepted.

Joe was escorted back to his cell. When I had calmed down a bit, I told my father that we had to speak to the prosecutor. I stormed into his office, followed by my poor father, and declared, "A court proceeding like this could only happen during Hitler's rule." In response, the prosecutor shouted at me, "How could such a good-looking young girl as you marry a dirty Jew?" He then turned on my father and asked, "How could you have allowed such a thing?" My father didn't understand what he was talking about, but I quickly realized that he must have confused me with Mrs. Blau. He knew that one of the wives of the sentenced men wasn't Jewish and he thought that I was the one. His error was the best thing that could have happened to us. I retorted, "This sentence, Comrade Prosecutor, will cost you dearly. You mixed us up. I am the dirty Jewess who married the Jew." I couldn't believe that antisemitism ran so deeply in Stalin's Communism that a prosecutor could publicly make such a racial slur. The prosecutor panicked and promised that he would remedy the situation. My father shook hands with him, but I walked out silently.

My father begged me to behave as we went into the office of the judge, Dr. Kobza, but there was no stopping me. I immediately went on the attack, asking, "What kind of judiciary are you representing? Yesterday you told us that my husband was coming home today and instead you personally pronounced a sentence of eight years." He apologized and admitted that just minutes before the trial the StB had instructed him to impose the sentence. This piece of information was another weapon in our hands and I told him that I would surely make use of it. He instantly regretted disclosing such guarded information and promised that he would help us by processing Joe's appeal in the shortest possible time.

I couldn't stop crying during the whole streetcar ride home. That evening, I suffered a severe gall bladder attack and had to be taken to the emergency ward for another shot of morphine. The next day, my father left for Bardejov. I had to go to work, so I was unable to take him to the railway station. I told everyone in my office that my husband had been sentenced to eight years and in sympathy they all cursed the entire Communist regime. I was completely exhausted and Vasek sent me home early that afternoon. When I got home I sat down and wrote a letter to Joe's sister, Aranka, in Canada and also enclosed a letter for her to forward to my uncle Bandi in Israel.[5] I gave them each a description of the situation in code. In the first letter I wrote, "To Aranka: The brother of Robert will be back for Tom's bar mitzvah" – Tom was five years old at that time and would reach thirteen after his father's eight-year sentence. I wrote a similarly coded message to Ruven. Then I called Uncle Jozko and told him the terrible news.

Several days after the trial, Tom returned from the convalescent home in Kynzvart. He looked healthy and had gained a lot of weight. I arranged for a neighbour to take care of Tom while I was at work during the day. She didn't work, as she had to take care of her mentally disabled child, who was approximately the same age as Tom.

The days were hard and seemingly endless. Many people warned us that we shouldn't have pursued the sentence through an appeal because it was possible that the judge would double Joe's prison time. My father persuaded me to move to Košice no matter what the outcome of the appeal. My brother, Ivan, was attending university there, and Uncle Sanyi and Aunt Lotte also lived in the same town. Being with family would help to ease the pain of my loneliness.

The appeal trial began in Prague in the first week of April and my father and Uncle Jozko attended the proceedings with me. I was less optimistic about the outcome than I had been at the first trial. I

---

5   Israel was considered to be a centre of subversive anti-Communist activity, therefore no one inside the Communist bloc could have any direct communication with people in Israel without arousing suspicions of treason.

prayed that the racial slur of the prosecutor and the stupidity of the judge would help us against the odds. It did appear to help a little – the sentence was reduced from eight years to six, with the additional proviso that after serving three of those years, Joe could apply for conditional release. It was still a pretty grim prospect.

When we got back to my apartment, my father, uncle and I decided not to delay my moving to Košice any longer. My father managed to find us shared accommodations and left with Tom so that I could move my furniture and belongings. Katka was still in Levice. We agreed that they would bring both the children to me after I moved. Tom cried – he didn't want to leave without me, but we assured him that we would all be together again within a few days.

The next day I went to work and informed them that I would be leaving within a week. We cried together and shared our hopes that one day there would be an end to the Communist regime and we would be able to read Masaryk openly. Vasek told me that there were several anti-Communist companies throughout Czechoslovakia. I thanked him for his patience and goodwill, and for giving me new qualifications that I could put to good use in the future.

Many of my friends, especially the Grunfelds, opposed my decision to leave. Eliska's husband, Paul, promised that he would be a substitute father to Tom and Katka and that Eliska would take care of my children while I worked. Their children were the same age as mine. It was a very generous offer, but I had already made up my mind. I explained to them that I was lonely and that my decision to move was final.

After the original trial, the Prague newspaper *Evening Prague* had published a sensationalized article about Joe and Mr. Blau's trial and subsequent sentencing. Seeing that was more than I could bear and I sped up my departure.

After my firm decision to move to Košice, the frightened prosecutor helped me arrange a visit with Joe, who was serving his sentence in a jail called Pankrác, which had actually been a detention camp for

Jews during the war. He looked even worse than he had at the trial. I asked Joe what he thought about us moving to Košice – I told him how alone I felt in Prague and that in Košice, Ivan would move in to help with the children and Uncle Sanyi and Aunt Lotte would be living close by. I begged him to take care of himself and assured him that I had a strong feeling that we would be together again in three years. I promised him that I would visit him every three months – the maximum number that was allowed.

I was very short of money. When I went to the railway station to arrange the freight delivery of the furniture, paintings and the rest of our belongings, I didn't have enough money to insure our meagre possessions. I had to sign documents stating that I would take full responsibility for the possibility of damage and prayed to God for protection.

I had three days to pack everything and prepare for the collection of our belongings. I called the Grunfelds for help and they arrived within half an hour. I thanked them, kissed them and begged them to understand my decision. I also went to say goodbye to Joe's colleagues and his previous boss, Ing Dolidze, and bid one last farewell to my colleagues and friends at Zasklivaci služba hlavního města Prahy. On April 26, 1956, I left Prague – I never lived there again.

Three Dark Years

Uncle Sanyi, Aunt Lotte and Ivan were waiting for me at the railway station in Košice when I arrived. They were shocked at my appearance – I had lost at least forty pounds. My new apartment was in an excellent location, although it was a shared apartment with a common corridor and bathroom. Our immediate neighbours, the Jirouts, were a little older than I was. The husband was a violinist in broadcasting – he played for a radio orchestra – and his wife stayed home to look after their two children, Janka and Milan, who were a little older than Tom and Katka. The family came from the Czech part of Czechoslovakia – the western part of the country that encompassed Bohemia and Moravia – and were quiet and clean people. My furniture hadn't arrived yet, so Uncle Sanyi brought Ivan and me two mattresses, along with some pillows and bedding.

Our apartment's windows faced the main square, Lenin's square, and four days after we moved in was May 1, a major Communist holiday.[1] We watched from our windows as thousands of people marched and celebrated their wonderful Communist achievements, which I

---

[1] Also known as International Workers' Day, May Day is celebrated on May 1 in many countries around the world in recognition of the achievements of workers and the international labour movement. For more information, see the glossary.

despised. After the parade, I got such a high fever that Ivan had to call an ambulance to take me to the hospital, where an old friend, Dr. Robert Skala, examined me. He explained that my high fever was due to gall bladder inflammation. He admitted me to the hospital and ordered me not to move from my bed. The treatment was a course of streptomycin, which at the time was an experimental medication with the danger of causing deafness.

It was a desolate beginning – instead of looking for a job and being with my children, I was forced to stay in the hospital. Ivan and I had made arrangements with Jozko and my father that immediately after my furniture arrived, they would bring the children to me. I couldn't wait until they came. I felt that my frequent gall bladder attacks were from the stress of not having my children with me, and that when they arrived, I would be healthy again.

After I'd been in hospital for three days, Uncle Sanyi and Ivan came to see me with excellent news: my furniture and belongings had arrived from Prague in good order and they had already furnished my apartment. Right away I asked Dr. Skala how long I would have to stay in the hospital. Unfortunately, he told me that the treatment cycle was ten days and since I still had a fever, I would have to stay for at least seven more days.

Two days later, my father arrived with Tom for a visit. Children weren't allowed inside the hospital, so I asked Dr. Skala if I could sit on a bench outside to see him. It was a warm spring day, so he thought it would be fine. To my delight, when I got outside I found not only my father and Tom, but my uncle and my little Katka, who had just turned two. She was holding hands with Uncle Jozko and Tom, and then, suddenly, she let go and ran toward me. Two months before, when I was in Levice, she hadn't even recognized me, but now she was calling, "Mami, Mami!" I couldn't lift her because I was so weak, but from the moment she hugged me, I knew that I couldn't leave her. I only had my nightgown on, but I was worried that if I went back into the hospital, the doctor would refuse to let me leave, so I just left all my clothes behind, got into a taxi with my children and went home. Tom and Katka held onto me tightly. My father and uncle admonished me that running away from a hospital was irresponsible, but I didn't care – I left them behind, asking them to tell the hospital staff that I'd gone home. Soon after I got there, my father and uncle arrived with Dr. Skala, who tried to persuade me to go back to the hospital. If I didn't, he said, he was sure that I wouldn't be able to avoid having surgery. But I had made up my mind – now that I had my children with me, I wasn't going to let anybody take me away from them again.

Three days later, my father and Uncle Jozko returned to Bardejov and Levice respectively, leaving me alone with Tom, Katka and Ivan. I was beyond thrilled to be reunited with my children – Katka held onto me every night as she slept in Joe's bed beside mine, and Tom slept in the crib close to my bed. I gave Katka the nickname "Kangaroo." With my children close to me, I was convinced that I was getting better. I didn't have any more gall bladder attacks.

I had to look for a job, but the process wasn't as difficult as it had been in Prague because I now had accounting experience. Within a few days I started a new job with a relatively high salary at a company called UMDEK. A friend of mine, Dr. Tibor Vozar, was the pediatrician in a very well-run daycare for children from wealthy families and arranged a place for Katka there. Tom started in a pre-school kindergarten.

On the first day that I took Katka to daycare, she cried inconsolably. The nurses were sure that she would adjust within a few days and encouraged me to leave her with them. They were mistaken, however, and in the end I had to take Katka out of this privileged nursery. I had to find some other arrangement, so Aunt Lotte introduced me to a Mrs. Litvay who looked after between three and five children. She was an exceptional person who was like a grandmother to the children and Katka felt immediately at ease with her. When he wasn't in school, I placed Tom with her too. Being a single mother was very difficult and this was an ideal solution since Mrs. Litvay could take care of the children even when they were sick. Unfortunately, this was quite often.

A few weeks had gone by when I got a phone call from my friend Eliska Grunfeld, telling me that she had just returned from Mrs. Sobel's funeral. Mrs. Sobel's husband had been there in handcuffs, accompanied by two prison guards. Hundreds of Jewish mourners were present. Mrs. Sobel's sister had told Eliska that two days earlier her sister had been harassed by the StB for being involved in distributing money to the families of Jewish prisoners and they were about to arrest her. She had suffered an emotional breakdown and, in front of her daughter, had jumped to her death from a ninth-floor window. The little girl ran into the corridor crying for help, but it was too late. Many families like the Sobels were destroyed by trumped-up charges for "crimes" that were invented or exaggerated by the Communist regime.

I learned much later that Mrs. Sobel's little girl had been raised by her aunt until her father was released from prison several years after her mother's death. He had been held only on the suspicion that he had connections to Zionist organizations abroad. In 1964, two or three years after his release, Dr. Sobel immigrated to Israel with his little girl and the family of his late wife's sister.

~

Tom and Katka ended their prayers every night with the words, "God help us that our father should return soon." Katka, being so young at the time, certainly couldn't have remembered her father, but she promised me that when she met him, she would kiss him.

As I had promised, I travelled to Prague every three months to visit Joe during those difficult years, even though it was an ordeal to schedule the trips. After work, I would leave Tom and Katka with Mrs. Litvay for two nights, stop off at home, pick up my little suitcase and go to the railway station. The train trip from Košice to Prague was a gruelling, twelve-hour ride. The train left at seven in the evening and arrived at seven in the morning, and I could only afford to travel third-class.

My visits with Joe were usually scheduled at ten o'clock in the morning. Before the visit, I would go to a fast-food snack place and then head to the prison building by streetcar. After a few formalities, I would be shown into a visiting room where Joe would be waiting for me, accompanied by two guards. We were allowed to visit for thirty minutes and had to watch every word because our conversations were monitored. In the first two years, we could only see each other through wire mesh in the presence of the two prison guards. It was painful every time our visit was terminated; our goodbyes were always agonizing for both of us.

On each visit to Prague, I went to see both the prosecutor and the judge to remind them about their promise to release Joe by the end of 1958. I also reminded them that I would publicize their racist statements if they resisted. I wasn't sure if this threat would have any real effect, but I hoped that it might unsettle them just enough to help me. I was quite sure that they would keep their word and that Joe would be released after three years, although Joe himself was pessimistic about the chances of that. The only bright spot amidst all the gloom was that Joe had found a way to work as a design engineer from within the prison walls. Although he had originally been assigned to menial work, plucking feathers for pillows, the guards soon found out about his expertise in engineering and he was sent to work in the design institute that the government had created inside the prison. The Technical Institute of the Ministry of the Interior paid him for sixteen hours of work a day, seven days a week. Two-thirds of his salary was deducted for his "food and accommodations" and the remaining one-third of his salary, which he sent to us, really helped.

After my visit with Joe, I usually went to see my former colleagues at Prague Glazing Services, as well as Ing Dolidze and a few other friends. At the end of the day, I would return to the railway station and take the train back to Košice, enduring another twelve hours of travel. When I arrived in Košice at seven in the morning, I would rush over to Mrs. Litvay's place to see the children before going to work. I would shower there and then hurry to the office. After work, I would pick up the children. Exhausted and overwhelmed, we would all go home to bed.

The children were permitted to visit Joe once a year. These emotionally devastating visits were also limited to thirty minutes, but the first time that the children went, the visit was somewhat more humane – Joe and the children were allowed to touch hands in the presence of the guards. Tom recognized his father immediately and held his hand, but Katka, sadly, refused to talk to him. After we left, I expressed my disappointment in her behaviour and reminded her of her prayers that her father would return soon. She replied, "I've seen my father now, but I will behave better when we visit God." In her two-year-old mind, when she had said her prayers, both God and her father had been equally abstract concepts.

On another occasion when I took the children to Prague by third-class train from Košicc, someone told me that the trip would be easier if I took a sleeping net that could be suspended from the ceiling. I did so and the next time we travelled I put Tom in the net and held Katka on my lap. The compartment was packed, with five people sitting on each side. By eleven at night almost everybody was asleep. Suddenly, at midnight, people jumped up from their seats, shouting, "What's going on?" Tom, sound asleep in the net swinging above us, was peeing and had wet everyone on either side of him. The passengers were certainly not very happy with me!

Although my trips to Prague were extremely hectic, my daily routine in Košice was just as busy. I worked from six o'clock in the morning to two in the afternoon, so I had to wake up Tom and Katka at five o'clock to take them by streetcar to Mrs. Litvay's place and still make it to work on time. I would pick them up at three in the afternoon and take them to the park and playground. Then I would have to do my grocery shopping, waiting in long lineups, before going home to prepare dinner. While I was cooking, Tom and Katka would play in the courtyard of the apartment building with the other children. At about six o'clock they would have dinner and a bath, and by seven they were in bed. After the children fell asleep, I would have to clean up the apartment, do the laundry by hand and iron the clothes. By nine o'clock at night I was exhausted. We didn't have any television to take my mind off my situation. I would talk with Ivan for a little while and then go to sleep. The next day I would start all over again. The winters were more strenuous than the summers because the heating system in my building was quite primitive. Every day, I had to carry coal up three flights of stairs. This hardship added to my ongoing health issues.

In the summer of 1957, my health started to deteriorate again and my gall bladder attacks increased. I lost more weight and my family doctor, Dr. Arpad Schweitzer – who was from Lučenec, the same town as my father – called my father after he had examined me. He told my father that if he didn't take me to his home for a few weeks' rest, he might end up caring for his grandchildren by himself. "She cannot go on this way any longer," he insisted.

My father arrived in Košice the next day and told me that I would have to take three weeks off work. He had arranged for my stepmother to take care of us to help my recovery. This was quite a change – before this he hadn't been able to persuade her to invite us even for a weekend. I managed to get the three weeks off work with the help of a medical certificate. I packed up some of our belongings – Katka was still in diapers at night – as well as valuable presents such as wool and coffee for my stepmother and stepgrandmother that I had received from relatives in Canada and the United States. We left for Bardejov by train with my father that same day.

As soon as we arrived at my father's house I could see that, except for the dog, Tarzan, nobody welcomed us. We were there for a total of three days. On the second day, when my father went to work, while

I was boiling Katka's cloth diapers, my stepmother began to shout at me, "You are here to ruin our lives!" She made it clear that she didn't want us in their home. When my father returned from work, I told him that it had been a bad idea to bring us there. I said that I was going to go back to Košice because my stepmother had threatened that if I didn't she would avoid me by going to the hospital. My father was so upset that he shouted at my stepmother, "Now the cup is overflowing. I have allowed your mother to live here for fifteen years, treating her with complete respect. I saved her life during the war, and now you are not willing to tolerate my sick daughter with my two grandchildren for three weeks? Now both of you get lost and get out of my house!" I was very upset and my gall bladder flared up again.

That evening my father sat beside me while I put the children to bed. Then he went to sleep, but not in his own bedroom. The next morning, before going to work, he brought me and the children breakfast in bed. He told me that he would always stand by me and asked me to disregard my stepmother and stepgrandmother. Nonetheless, that night I decided not to stay in their house any longer. After my father left for work the next morning, I dressed the children, packed our most important belongings and left the rest there.

Before leaving, I wrote a letter to my father, thanking him for his loving support. I also wrote that his place was beside his wife and mother-in-law and that it had been a bad idea for me to come to a home in which I didn't belong. I asked him to come to Košice on the weekend and bring the rest of my belongings. Most importantly, I wrote, he should stay calm. I implored him to understand the reason for our departure, that it was the only solution to a difficult situation. I didn't want to say goodbye to my stepgrandmother and my stepmother. My room was only about five feet above the ground and there was a tree in front of the window. Tom went out first. When he had landed safely on the ground, I handed him one suitcase and then Katka; I climbed out last. We walked the fifteen minutes to the railway station and waited an hour for the next train. I couldn't help crying on our way back to Košice, but I hid my face from the children. Katka didn't understand what was happening; for Tom, it was all a great adventure.

When we got back to Košice, I went to Aunt Lotte and Uncle Sanyi for moral support; at home, I also told Ivan about what had happened in Bardejov. He was loyal to me and didn't visit his mother and grandmother for quite awhile after that. Whatever had happened after my father returned from work and found that I had left must have been dramatic because he moved out of the house for about three months. Two days after our return, he showed up in Košice. He wasn't pleased with my decision to leave Bardejov, but he tried to understand it. After my three weeks' leave was up, I returned to work a little more relaxed. My family doctor advised me to gain weight and asked a psychiatrist, Dr. Ivan Major, to counsel me and also treat me with insulin shots to improve my appetite.

In the meantime, I continued to fight for Joe's release; I submitted several petitions for clemency, all to no avail. The news I received from reliable sources was discouraging – apparently, Joe wouldn't be released, as I had been led to believe, because of his position as an engineer for the Ministry of the Interior. They would fight to keep him there since they didn't have a replacement. Still, I didn't give up hope.

One day, I was walking on Main Street with Tom and Katka when a photographer approached me and asked if he could take a photo of Katka for an advertisement for the first children's beauty salon in Košice. In return, he promised to give me a free photograph and a free haircut. I agreed, but only if he agreed to take pictures of each of my children. A few days later, the photographs showed up on a huge, rotating billboard on Main Street with the following headline: "The Happy Children of Socialism." I was not amused. I went to the mayor of Košice to protest this deception. The only good that came of it was that the mayor helped me submit a petition for Joe's release. This effort, however, was not successful. I could see that my fight against the Communist establishment would be exceedingly difficult.

At work, I got another taste of how the system operated. One day, my colleague, Marta Farkas, and I were asked to bring some invoices to a branch where an inspector from Bratislava was carrying out an investigation. When we arrived, to our horror, we saw the two employees under investigation beating the inspector, who was lying on the floor bleeding. Throughout the assault the two men shouted, "You damned Jews, you all returned from the concentration camps where they should have killed you all, but it's never too late. We'll finish the job." I ran outside and flagged down a policeman, who stopped the brutality.

When the case came to court, I was the main prosecution witness. I had to testify about both the racial slurs and the bloody beating. The outcome of the trial was typical for the antisemitic environment we were living in – the judge freed the two thugs and the inspector lost his job. It was outrageous. I was so disgusted with my employers at UMDEK that I quit, in spite of my decent salary. With the help of the manager of the health department, Dr. Bertekap, I got a new position in a branch for disease prevention under the guidance of Dr. Fahidi. It was interesting work, but with a much lower pay than I had had before. I could manage my expenses only because of the money I was receiving from Joe's salary.

Our lives continued to be plagued by one mishap after another. Tom accidentally dropped a steel frame on Katka's foot, which had to be put in a cast. This was just before their annual visit to Prague and I had to take her to visit Joe with her foot in a cast. Around that same time, Tom broke his arm playing hockey. He also still had frequent bouts of tonsillitis. I was advised to have his tonsils removed, so I took advantage of my work connections at the health department. Professor Schuster, who was considered to be the best in this field, carried out the surgery successfully and Tom's health improved.

When I went to pick up Katka on Saturday June 14, 1957, Mrs. Litvay greeted me with some very distressing news. She told me that Katka had a high fever, was vomiting and had such strong headaches that she couldn't move her head. Although I hadn't finished my medical education, I still recognized the symptoms of meningitis, and worried that Katka might have it. I called Dr. Vozar right away and, on hearing her symptoms, he confirmed my fears. Because it was Saturday, we would have to wait until Monday morning to arrange a lumbar puncture, a very intricate procedure that could only be performed by a highly specialized doctor; only interns worked in the hospital on the weekends. It was anguish to see Katka suffering. We couldn't touch her head and had to carry her in our arms. Dr. Vozar prescribed some medication to treat the headaches and nausea over the weekend. She vomited constantly and couldn't keep anything in her stomach.

My friend Edith Ivascu arrived to stay with us until Monday morning and Dr. Vozar came to see Katka on Sunday. He wanted to send her to the hospital because she was so dehydrated, but I begged him to hold off until Monday morning. On Sunday night, Katka fell asleep in my arms and I placed her beside me in the bed. I was completely exhausted. Before I fell asleep, I called on my mother to save my little girl and give me another miracle. On Monday morning, June 16 – my birthday – Katka woke up and and kissed me. She said, "Look, Mami, my head doesn't hurt anymore. Give me my bottle, I'm hungry." She even jumped out of bed. My friend came into the room, amazed, and remarked, "This is a miracle! I don't think that we have to go to the hospital." But, of course, I did still have to go to the hospital since a team of doctors was waiting to carry out the lumbar puncture.

When we got to the hospital, Dr. Vozar was already there, along with Mrs. Litvay, who was in tears. Katka was crying because she was hungry – she had absolutely no signs of fever, neck pain or vomiting. Dr. Vozar also proclaimed it to be a miracle. He cancelled the whole procedure and told me to give her lots of fluid and to keep him informed about her condition. This was the best present I could have hoped for on my birthday.

After this happy ending, I took Katka to Mrs. Litvay's place. It was only then that she admitted to me something that she hadn't wanted to tell me earlier. They had a peach tree in the backyard, but in June the peaches weren't ripe yet. On that fateful Saturday Katka had been playing with the children in the back and had eaten quite a few of the unripe peaches. By the time the older children told her what had happened, it was too late. She didn't know what the consequences might be. She was a simple, good-hearted woman. Had she told me the truth that same day, I wouldn't have overreacted and suspected meningitis; we could have prevented all the terrifying events of the weekend. But despite this one mishap, she was my lifesaver. She took care of both children whenever I needed her to, which was quite often. She even came to our home to take care of them. I don't know how I would have survived without her. I bless her to this day.

～

While Joe was still incarcerated I made friends with some of the women whose husbands were also engineers and worked with Joe in prison, including a woman named Babec Zalobin. Ironically, these women were a group of devoted Catholics – I was their only Jewish friend – but they accepted me into their inner circle and we were all close friends for a long time. We spent a lot of time together and could understand each other since we lived under similar circumstances. The group had a patron by the name of Jan Mathé, a well-known sculptor.[2] He was our advisor and protector.

One day, I received a notice from the post office to pick up some money. It was a huge amount, but the sender was unknown. I was alarmed and recalled my visits to the prosecutor, who had warned me not to make any mistakes. Although I needed the money desperately,

---

2   Jan Mathé was a prominent Slovak sculptor who had been very involved with Prague's Catholic academic community before the Communist coup and continued to quietly oppose Communism afterwards, resisting any pressure to follow the socialist-realist art style dictated by the Communist regime.

I was wary of entrapment and handed it over to the police. This mysterious event occurred four or five more times, and on each occasion, I gave the money to the police. I never did find out who the money was from.

In the spring of 1958, I received a phone call at work from a caller who introduced himself as engineer Drahovsky and told me that he was in daily contact with my husband. He said that he worked as a civil liaison for Chemoprojekt Prague and the design institute inside the prison. He told me that Joe was working on the design of a power station in Likier, a small town about one hundred kilometres from Košice. He said he would be there the next day, staying at the local hotel, and that I could meet him there with my children. Drahovsky said he would take me to the power station where Joe had a consultation that day – he was going to be in Likier to attend an important meeting with the principals of the power station. He said that he had children of his own and that was why he wanted to do this favour for us; he assured me that it would be an extraordinary visit. I thanked him and told him that I would try to come.

I asked several people for advice, including my father. Everybody was opposed to my going, warning me that it could be a serious trap. But I was determined to go and asked Aunt Lotte to help me get the children ready. On top of everything else, I found out that the railway connection was really complicated – the train was scheduled to leave at six o'clock in the morning and we would have to make two transfers; the travel time was four hours each way. The stress of all this brought on another major gall bladder attack that evening and, once again, the doctor had to come and give me a morphine shot. Aunt Lotte told me that I would have to cancel the trip, that I wasn't well enough to travel, and left. But I had my own plans. I fell asleep and woke at four o'clock in the morning, got the children up, dressed them, prepared some food and chocolate milk and walked the twenty minutes to the railway station.

The children slept on the train. At one point I got frightened and wondered whether I was doing the right thing in undertaking such a trip. It could be a trap – after all, this visit wasn't exactly legal. We arrived in Likier and I easily found the hotel. There were a lot of people in the reception area. A man approached me and introduced himself as Ing Drahovsky. I asked him how he knew who I was and he said that he had seen photos of the children on Joe's desk. He invited us to sit down at a table and ordered lunch. While we were waiting for our food to come, Drahovsky said that he realized that he had made a mistake in asking me to come. In the first place, he hadn't realized that Košice was so far away. More importantly, when he had told Joe that he had arranged a wonderful surprise for him – that he had already contacted me by telephone to confirm that all three of us would be arriving to visit him – Joe had told him how illegal such a visit was and that the prison authorities would never allow it. Joe was really concerned that the whole scheme would be very damaging to all of us.

Drahovsky didn't want my whole journey to be a waste, so he thought, at the very least, that he could arrange for Joe to see us through the ground floor windows that faced the street. After lunch, Drahovsky took us outside to the window where Joe would be seated and then left. I told Tom that when he saw his father through the window, he shouldn't wave at him because it was very dangerous. I wasn't worried about Katka having any reaction because she still didn't really remember her father.

I played with the children close to the window, throwing little stones into puddles, and after few minutes, I saw Joe's face appear. I wanted him to see us. To my surprise, after about five minutes, Joe himself suddenly walked outside, calling, "Agika, Tomasku, Katka!" I was really flustered, unsure of what to do and how to act. At that point, one of the guards called us in. He had seen Joe crying, unable to hide his emotion at seeing us. He had told the guards that his wife and children were outside and, fortunately, these particular guards were decent people who had children of their own – they allowed us to spend an hour with Joe. The guards asked us never to tell anyone that such a visit had taken place. One of them even gave Katka pocket money – he had a daughter the same age. It was the nicest, most private visit we'd had with Joe and Katka kissed her father for the first time in two and a half years.

I assured Joe that I was positive he would be home before the year was out. He wasn't as optimistic, saying that he had information to the contrary. He felt that his expertise in design was making the authorities very unwilling to release him. After a heart-wrenching goodbye, we left to travel back to Košice. I arrived home with the children close to midnight, tired but elated that my intuition had been correct.

One day in the summer of 1958 I was walking on Main Street in Košice with Babec Zalobin and Jano Mathé when I suddenly spotted Joe's prosecutor from Prague, Dr. Siegel. I asked my friends to wait for me, saying, "There's the prosecutor from Prague. I have to talk to him." Surprisingly, Dr. Siegel was actually pleased to see me, asking right away whether the man I was with was my boyfriend. I replied, "You are mistaken – Jewish wives are faithful to their 'dirty Jewish men.'" I asked him what he was doing in Košice and he explained that as the highest representative from Prague, he was presiding over the graduation of the newly appointed prosecutors. He flattered me, telling me how good-looking I was, and asked me to meet him that evening in the cafeteria of the Hotel Slovan, where he was staying. I agreed.

When we parted, I relayed the whole conversation to Jano and Babec. Jano didn't want to let me go to the meeting alone and insisted on going with me. He said that he would sit at the table closest to ours. My conversation with Dr. Siegel focused on his promise to help get Joe released before the end of that year – the earliest possible date for a legal release. The political climate was milder now and antisemitism had begun to decline somewhat.[3] That gave me even more cour-

---

3 Following Stalin's death in 1953, Soviet leader Nikita Khrushchev denounced Stalin and his crimes in a 1956 "secret speech" to the Party congress, which led to

age to demand that he keep his promise. Hoping it would work to my advantage, I repeated my threat that if he failed to cooperate with me he would face the consequences of having his racist statements publicized. He shook my hand and promised that he would do whatever he could to help get Joe released. At the same time, however, he reminded me that he wasn't necessarily the one who made the final decision. I was sure that this accidental meeting would decide our fate – that Joe would be home within a few months.

My next visit to Joe was in September 1958. I told him that this would be my last visit to the prison since he would be home in three months. He was still positive that it wouldn't happen that soon. Once again, I went to the prosecutor and the judge, and they both assured me that the application for Joe's half-term release would be submitted shortly.

When I got back to Košice, our routine went on as before. The days went by painstakingly slowly. I was still experiencing gall bladder attacks and the doctors were advising me to have the surgery. As a single mother, however, it was a luxury I couldn't afford. I was positive that Joe would be back in a few months and then I would be able to focus on my health. My father visited us every two weeks, bringing sweets covered in chocolate for the children. In December 1958, he came to tell me he had made arrangements with my stepmother for us to spend the three days of the New Year's holidays together. This time he would come and stay in our home, so our last visit's ugly ending would not be repeated. Ivan wanted us to go with him to Bardejov, but I refused, still adamant that Joe would be home soon.

On December 23, 1958, Ivan took Tom with him to Bardejov for a visit before Christmas. I stayed in Košice with Katka, against my

---

a general thaw (known as "destalinization") throughout the Soviet bloc, including Czechoslovakia. By 1957, a small minority of the political sentences that had been imposed in prior years began to be reversed or reduced.

father's and Ivan's wishes. That evening a telegram arrived, advising me to go to the post office immediately and call a certain phone number (we didn't have a telephone at home). I woke up our neighbour, Mr. Jirout, and asked him to escort me to the post office; it was late at night and the post office was quite far away – I was afraid to go alone. I asked Mrs. Jirout to babysit Katka while we went. When I called the number, I discovered that it belonged to distant relatives of ours, Pali and Katka Knopfelmacher, who told me that Joe was free! He had gone to their apartment to get in touch with me and then had left for the railway station to catch the last train to Košice. The train would be leaving at ten o'clock that night and would arrive in Košice at ten the next morning. I cried out with excitement, overjoyed that Joe was finally free. I wanted them to repeat their message over and over. I asked them for more details, so they told me that Joe had been released that same day, December 23, 1958, at approximately three in the afternoon. He had gone straight from the court to buy presents for the children. He had bought Tom some sort of a car and Katka a doll with eyes that opened and closed.

After this exhilarating conversation, I immediately sent a telegram to Bardejov to ask Ivan and my father to bring Tom back to Košice right away. My joy was indescribable. I woke up Katka to tell her that her father was coming home in the morning. Katka, at four and a half, didn't quite understand what was going on. I couldn't fall asleep so I began preparing food. In the morning, I went to tell Aunt Lotte and Uncle Sanyi the good news; they came to the railway station with me and Katka. It's hard to describe what it was like getting through the hours before the train arrived. When it finally pulled up and we saw Joe with a big box and a little suitcase in his hands, I couldn't contain my tears of joy.

Three hours after we got home, Tom, my father and Ivan arrived from Bardejov. Everyone was crying. A traumatic and difficult chapter of our life was finally coming to an end. We had overcome all the hardships of these last three years because we were very young. At the end of this dark period of our lives, I was only twenty-eight years old and had an indomitable will to fight against the odds. I hadn't given up, even when my fight had appeared hopeless.

Our dream of reuniting came true on December 24, 1958. I had a strong feeling that Joe and I would be on a new course toward a happier life. We hoped to protect our children from the hardships we had endured, and we also hoped that one day, with God's help, we would leave this country behind.

Time to Leave

Now that we were reunited as a family, we were optimistic about the future. Our first surprise, however, was Katka's reaction to her father's return. She had slept next to me in the twin bed every night during the three years that Joe was interned, but on his first night back, as soon as she had fallen asleep in her usual spot curled up with the beautiful new doll he had given her, we moved her into one of the cribs in our room. When we woke up the next morning, we discovered that she had put the doll back in its box. We asked her what she was doing and she replied, "Mami, I'd rather give up the doll and send him back to Prague. I want my bed back." It took a while before she got used to the fact that her father was going to stay. She kept trying to either send him back or convince him to sleep in the crib so she could keep the doll. Joe eventually persuaded her that her crib was too small for him.

Our next priority was to find Joe a job in his profession. Job hunting wasn't easy for him in early 1959 because of the slow and stilted economic situation in Czechoslovakia under Communism. Due to his excellent reputation, he finally got a job as a design engineer with a company called Hutné Stavby Development, where he was promoted several times. That same year I had the gall bladder surgery that I hadn't been able to afford when I was a single mother. Having neglected my gallstones for so long, I woke up one morning with severe jaundice and acute pain. My whole body was as yellow as a canary. We rushed to the hospital, where I had to have emergency surgery. Such a complicated procedure was very risky at that time but I had the best possible surgeon, Dr. Bardos. He removed twenty-six large gallstones and I had to have a tube to remove bile inserted in me for over three weeks. I felt so sick and weak that when my children came to visit me in the hospital, I was worried that I wouldn't be around to raise them. I will never forget the terror in their eyes when they saw me.

With God's help, I gradually recovered. I went to Karlovy Vary spa several times for treatment in the healing mineral springs and my health improved. I continued to work in the very rewarding field of health prevention, but I had already decided to become a registered nurse. I started my college education in 1960 and graduated with honours as a registered nurse in 1962. With my newly obtained nursing diploma, I got a job in a school doing preventive medicine with adolescent youth. My boss was Dr. Reichard, who lived in our neighbourhood.

The same year that I started my nursing program, my father had a heart attack and had to stay in hospital for six weeks. I travelled from Košice to Bardejov every week to visit him. Two weeks after his heart attack, my father's older brother, Uncle Joska, died suddenly of a heart attack in Budapest. His wife, Margit, came to stay with us to recuperate from the shock. I asked everybody in the family to keep the news of his brother's death from my father while his own health was so fragile. But I made a terrible slip of the tongue while visiting my father in the hospital the next day. I told him that Aunt Margit was staying with us and when he asked how she looked, I responded, "Can you imagine her dressed all in black?" My father immediately exclaimed, "Oh my God, my brother is dead!" I had to call for help from the doctor, who gave him a tranquilizer to calm him down.

Despite these ups and downs, our family life was beginning to get back to normal. Ivanko followed in our father's footsteps and finished his dental certification in Košice in 1960. In 1961 he married Hedika Bergmann and they had a child, Ivetka, on June 1, 1962. When Ivan and I got home from the hospital, he told Tom and Katka that they had a new cousin and that the stork had dropped her down the chimney. Tom's response to that was to say, "Ivan, you were the stork and Hedika was the chimney." Ivanko had clearly forgotten that Tom was now eleven years old and understood more than Ivan gave him credit for!

Joe and I decided that our children had musical talent. Tom started out playing the violin and then switched to piano. When he decided that he would rather play the guitar, Joe went to his music teacher and asked which instrument he thought Tom should specialize in. The teacher replied, "Tom should specialize in swimming." Katka was also taking piano lessons without great results, although we had bought a Rossler, the best piano available. She did, with great difficulty, manage to finish four years of piano school, but we had to promise the piano teacher that if she passed the last year, we wouldn't push her to continue. So much for our children's "successes" in the musical field.

We had a few problems with Tom around this time. Working in the health care field gave me the opportunity to get Tom a place in a special summer camp in Krompachy, a town in the scenic mountain region of northeast Slovakia. At eleven years old, Tom was still a poor eater and extremely thin – the focus of the camp was to help improve children's health. After only three days there, however, Tom ran away; he didn't like being away from us. Everyone searched high and low for him, to no avail. It turned out that Tom had decided to take the train to Košice and when we got home from work later that day we were shocked to find him waiting for us at the front door. We were really upset and told Tom in no uncertain terms that his behaviour was reprehensible. The police arrived and notified the camp that they had located Tom and would be bringing him back the next day. I decided that it would be better if I took him myself, so the next day I went back to the camp with him by train. He wasn't very happy about it but was relieved that he didn't have to return with a police escort.

But that wasn't the end of the story. When Joe and I got back from work the following day, Uncle Sanyi was waiting there for us with the startling news that Tom was at their place. He had run away again, but this time was careful to outsmart the police. Instead of going straight to Košice, he had gotten off the train in Barca, about four kilometres away, and walked to Uncle Sanyi's place. Mr. Zalobin, a close friend of ours who had three sons, was there when Uncle Sanyi told us about Tom's latest escape. He thought that we should bring Tom home and give him a good thrashing to discourage this behaviour. One day Tom would be obliged to serve in the military, he argued, and if he ever tried leaving there without permission, he would face grave consequences. We understood what he was saying, but we just couldn't bring ourselves to physically hurt our son – we let Zalobin beat him instead. It's a decision that I regret to this day. Tom never did go back to the camp that summer.

Katka also had a negative experience at summer camp one year; she came home with very swollen cheeks. We took her to our pediatrician, who told us that he couldn't tell what was going on without doing more tests. Katka was in a lot of pain. I didn't know enough medicine to be helpful and I started to panic, thinking about all the things that could possibly be wrong with her. Over the next five days, we visited lots of specialists. The swelling wasn't easing up at all, but the blood tests fortunately showed no infection, so we knew only that there was inflammation. One of the best pediatricians, Dr. Gerta Bardos, who was also a neighbour of ours, advised us to see a dentist to eliminate the possibility that the swelling was being caused by a problem with Katka's teeth.

To our bewilderment, the dentist advised us to have all of Katka's teeth pulled. But these were her permanent teeth so, of course, we refused. Ivanko was with us at the dentist's and suggested that we get another opinion. The ear, nose and throat specialist told us that we needed to have the pus drained from her jaw. After consulting with several other specialists, Dr. Bardos decided to apply a hot lubrication called Ichthyol.[1] Katka's pain got even worse during the treatment, so Joe decided that all the doctors were incompetent and administered ice packs instead. I strongly disagreed with him, but he insisted. He personally changed these cold compresses over and over again into the wee hours of the morning, by which time Katka's pain and swelling had gradually subsided. When she awoke, she was completely free of pain and the swelling was all gone.

Katka had another more positive camping experience a few years later when her whole class went to a summer camp twenty kilometres from Košice for three days. I took Katka to the school bus with her belongings in the morning before I went to work. She was very popular and when we arrived, her classmates cheered and welcomed us. All of a sudden, though, Katka didn't feel well. I wanted to take her home, as I worried we would have a repeat of her last camp experience, but the teacher assured us that everything would be fine.

I stood and watched until the bus left. I was so concerned about Katka that Tom, who didn't have any school that day, said, "Don't worry, Mami, I'll ride my bicycle to the camp to see how she's doing." By the time that I got home from work, Tom had already returned from the camp and assured me that Katka was happy and laughing and playing with the other children. I was so relieved. It was a wonderful thing that Tom did and I appreciated it very much.

We had another problem with Tom when he was about fifteen, though – he wasn't doing very well at school because he was spending most of his time playing sports. When he saw his report card at the end of the school year, he was worried about what Joe and I would

---

1   Also known as ammonium bituminosulfonate, Ichthyol is an ointment that has ant-inflammatory properties and is commonly used to treat abscesses and other skin problems such as acne and psoriasis.

say and decided not to come home. We still hadn't heard from him late in the evening and were extremely worried about him. My father – who was now living in Košice – Ivanko and Uncle Sanyi came over to help us decide what to do. We called the police and started looking for him everywhere possible. Nobody got any sleep and I spent the whole night shaking and crying. My father was so upset that he said I should give Tom a beating when he got home. It was daybreak before Tom finally came home from his wanderings in the parks, but instead of punishing him I kissed his cold feet, made him some hot chocolate and put him to bed. All my father could say was, "You're killing him with your excessive love."

We moved a lot in those years – during our ten years in Košice, we moved four times. Maybe it was because Joe was starting to get restless and was once again starting to talk about emigrating. At one point, Katka absolutely refused to change schools one more time and went to the school psychologist, Dr. Hvozdik, to complain about our constant moves. She enlisted his help and got permission to stay in the same school after one of our moves.

~

By the mid-1960s, the political situation in Czechoslovakia was shifting yet again and some restrictions were beginning to ease.[2] Constraints on travel were still being enforced, but we were now permitted to travel to the West as long as one spouse stayed behind, to

---

2   In 1960, Communist president Antonín Novotný introduced a new Czech constitution that simultaneously re-affirmed the state's commitment to Communism and also enacted a number of minor reforms designed to further the process of de-Stalinization – more political prisoners were given amnesty and previous restrictions on connections with and travel to the West were loosened. In conjunction with the new constitution's general reforms on religion – citizens were to be allowed a degree of religious freedom as long as doing so didn't contravene the laws of the state – Czech citizens were now permitted to travel to Israel.

ensure that the whole family didn't defect. We were even allowed to travel to Israel and Joe and I each travelled there separately in 1965 and 1966. My biggest trip was in 1966, when Tom and I went first to Athens, Greece where Joe's brother Robert and his family had a posting with the Israeli consulate. We had to spend two full days and nights in a third-class train to get there. We stayed in their home for two days – greatly admiring their lavish lifestyle – and then travelled on a cargo ship that was delivering mail to Haifa. Because the ship was small and there was no privacy, the men and women were separated, and I barely managed to get the crew to agree to let Tom, who was fifteen years old, stay with me. Israel impressed us very much – the standard of living was far higher than in Czechoslovakia – and I hoped that we would immigrate there one day. In 1967, Joe was also able to visit his sister, Aranka, in Canada for two months.

$\sim$

In 1968, the Communist Party of Czechoslovakia, under the leadership of Alexander Dubček, introduced a program of political liberalization and decentralization called "Socialism with a Human Face."[3] Among other aspects of this new program was a provision that many workers – including design engineers – were allowed to earn a second income in their off-hours. Joe took full advantage of this opportunity and began teaching at a college after work. Another change was that Czechoslovakian Jews were now permitted to apply to emigrate to Israel. Joe and I submitted an application but were turned down be-

---

3   Alexander Dubček was the Slovak politician who replaced Antonín Novotný as First Secretary of the Communist Party on January 5, 1968, and implemented a program of liberal reforms known as "The Prague Spring." The political and economic reforms implemented under Dubček's leadership resulted in greater freedom for Czech citizens. His April 1968 Action Program of democratic reforms, for example, included freedom of the press, freedom of speech and assembly, and greater freedom to travel. For more information, see the glossary.

cause Joe's job in the iron and steel works in Košice was considered essential to the economy. The factory in which he worked was enormous – it incorporated approximately two hundred buildings with four blast furnaces, rolling mills, a cokery and its own power plant – and was the main supply line for precast panels for the entire housing industry in Košice.

With the boost in our income from Joe's teaching, our lifestyle improved. Joe, Tom, Katka and I enjoyed various trips throughout Czechoslovakia and Hungary, where we could travel without any restrictions. We also took several ski holidays with my cousin, Katka, to the High and Low Tatra Mountains, and to Lake Balaton in Hungary. Katka's mother, Aunt Ica, had unfortunately passed away at the young age of fifty-eight.

Our last trip from Czechoslovakia was to Dubrovnik, Yugoslavia in August 1968 with our friends Arnost and Edith Zeman. Joe and I had finally been able to afford to buy a car the year before – our little Fiat 850 had cost us more than a year's income – and, since the Zemans also had a car, we drove in tandem, carrying tents and canned food. Even though Joe, the children and I all had to sleep together in a very small tent, we had a wonderful time.

We had been away for two weeks when Joe received a telegram instructing him to return to Košice immediately because his company was sending him to Sweden on a special assignment. He had participated in several international conferences on their behalf in Hungary, Poland, Russia and East Germany. Arnost and Edith set out on the return journey with us and when we all got to the border between Yugoslavia and Hungary, we heard over the radio that something dramatic was happening in Czechoslovakia. Tom begged us not to go back – many other people who were vacationing outside of Czechoslovakia during this critical period had decided to escape to the West through Yugoslavia and Austria. We, however, decided to return.

We arrived in Košice on August 20 and Joe left for Sweden with another colleague the same day. He stayed at the house of the factory owner, Mr. Johanson, at Björkvik, close to the port of Nyköping on the southeast coast of Sweden. At breakfast the next morning, on August 21, 1968, Joe saw a television news report showing tanks in the streets of Prague. The report was in Swedish, so Joe couldn't understand it, but commented to his host that they must be looking at a scene from the 1945 Soviet liberation of Prague. Mr. Johanson told him that he was seriously mistaken. They were watching a report that was being broadcast live from Prague – they were watching the current Soviet occupation of Czechoslovakia.[4]

Joe was completely cut off from us. The telephone lines weren't working and the Soviet army and its allies had occupied all the airports in Czechoslovakia, so there were no civilian flights in or out of the country. The next morning, news reporters arrived from Nyköping and besieged Joe with questions that he was afraid to answer. The following day, articles appeared in the Swedish newspapers with his photo, reporting that Czech engineers had been stranded in Sweden and separated from their families. The Swedish newsmen encouraged Joe to defect, but he refused to abandon us.

Meanwhile, Ivan called us in the middle of the night to tell me that Soviet tanks were rolling through the streets of Košice. I went to look out from our balcony and thought that a war had broken out. I woke the children, dressed them, grabbed some food and went to join Ivan and his family at my father's place. My father's reaction to these frightening events was to say, "This situation reminds me of

---

4 The Soviet government under Leonid Brezhnev strongly condemned the steps toward decentralization and liberalization inherent in the reforms initiated by Alexander Dubček. On August 21, 1968, armies from members of the Warsaw Pact – a mutual defense treaty signed by the USSR, Bulgaria, Poland, Hungary and East Germany – invaded Czechoslovakia and re-established an authoritarian Communist regime that reversed the liberal reforms that had been gained during the Prague Spring.

the arrival of the Germans in 1939." His statement made a lasting impression on me – at that moment I decided that we had to leave Czechoslovakia.

The next day, the children stayed with my father while Ivan and I went to work. There were some shooting incidents in the streets. The Czechoslovakian government was encouraging the population to peacefully demonstrate against the Soviet invaders, but it was getting increasingly difficult for them to get their message out – within three days the Soviets had occupied all the radio and television stations.[5] I respected the government's call to resistance a great deal, but I had already made up my mind to emigrate.

More and more people were leaving the country and so far the border authorities were letting them through. Ivan didn't want to leave at first, but Hedi persuaded him. We tried to convince my father and his wife to come with us, but my father simply said, "You cannot transplant an old tree." He had been sick for some time and was suffering from regular high fevers that the doctors couldn't seem to diagnose. My stepmother also had signs of Parkinson's disease. Despite all of this, my father heroically encouraged us to leave the country, declaring, "I know that you're leaving not because you don't love us, but because you want to secure a better future for your children."

It was two weeks before Joe could get a flight from Stockholm to Vienna and from there he took the train to Košice. We were happy to be reunited. Joe didn't think that it was smart for us to leave right away because he had seen that Vienna was already full of refugees. Nonetheless, my intuition was still strongly telling me to leave Czechoslovakia – throughout September I concentrated on speeding up our departure. The day before we left, Joe, Tom, Katka and I went

---

5   At the time of the Soviet invasion, the Czech Communist executive committee was in session, and though they condemned the occupation, they asked the public to avoid a violent confrontation. For the most part, Czech and Slovak citizens demonstrated peacefully against the Soviet occupation.

to the cemetery to say goodbye to my mother. I felt strongly that she blessed our decision and that she would be with us wherever we went.

Tom was excited about emigrating, but Katka cried because she wanted to stay. We told her that she had to keep the fact that we would be leaving soon a secret – her best friend's father was a prominent Communist and the authorities were starting to clamp down on emigration. We arranged our travel documents, sold our Fiat 850, packed two suitcases and told everyone that we were going to a wedding in Vienna. We had one last family celebration for my father's sixty-seventh birthday on October 16, 1968.

Leaving my father behind was heartbreaking. Dr. Bardos advised me to put my father in the hospital, where he would be in safe hands, and we decided to take his advice. Since Ivan and his family had left Košice the day before, I had to take him myself. It was a teary goodbye.

We had arranged to meet Ivan and his family in Bratislava. We didn't want to arouse any suspicions at the border, so when we left Bratislava on October 21, we divided into two groups for the trip. Ivan hadn't sold his car and drove to the Austrian border with Joe and Tom, while Katka, Hedika, Ivetka and I travelled by train. Crossing the border was dangerous and many people were being turned back. We agreed that if part of the family wasn't able to cross the border, we would all turn back. If either group was interrogated, we would tell the authorities that the other half of the family had stayed home.

The trip from Bratislava to Vienna only took an hour by car. When Katka, Hedika, Ivetka and I arrived at the train station, our friend Sanyi Vesely was waiting for us (he and his family had left the day before us, as had our friends the Gregors). He told us that Tom, Joe and Ivan had arrived safely. From that day on, I had the definite feeling that I was leading my children to a more hopeful, better future. October 21, 1968, marked the beginning of our new life – we had finally left the Iron Curtain behind.

Our family, Ivan's family, the Veselys and the Gregors all moved into Vienna's Apollo Hotel, which wasn't exactly luxurious. When we got to our room and unpacked our belongings, to our surprise Katka showed us a little present from her best friend, Viola Romankova, whose father was the high-ranking Communist official – despite our warnings, she had told her friend about our departure. We were extremely lucky that we hadn't been arrested in Košice.

Fortunately, our whole group was soon able to move together into more comfortable accommodations. Joe found a job right away with the Hebrew Immigrant Aid Society (HIAS) because of his knowledge of English and German.[6] Since Joe's sister, Aranka, lived in Canada and the country had a policy of welcoming Czechs who were escaping Communism, we applied to come to Canada as political refugees. Our group spent four weeks in Vienna, marking time until all the Canadian immigration formalities, such as medical screening and answering questions about our skills and education, had been completed. I was still preoccupied with having left my father behind and we went to the post office to call him almost every day.

After a month of waiting, the Canadian consulate gave us our airplane tickets – they were free of charge with our promise to repay them as soon as we were able. Our group arrived at Pearson International airport in Toronto on November 21, 1968, a historic day in the life of our family.

---

6 Founded in New York in 1881, the Hebrew Immigrant Aid Society provides aid, counsel, support and general assistance to Jewish immigrants all over the world.

A New Beginning

When we landed in Toronto, Joe's sister, Aranka, her son, Tomy, and Gordon Singer, one of Joe's colleagues from the University of Prague, met us at the airport and took us to our assigned accommodations at the Ford Hotel. The day we arrived was both snowy and rainy, and the Ford was a very substandard hotel, so our first impression of Toronto was depressing. On top of all this gloom, we learned that Aranka's husband, Fred, had suffered a massive heart attack just four days earlier and was in the intensive care unit. Aranka was extremely worried about him and was very concerned about their future. As new immigrants we didn't have much money or a permanent place to live, so we weren't in any position to help her. What was encouraging, however, was that Gordon Singer promised to help Joe find an engineering job.

Within three days of our arrival, we were all moved from the disastrous Ford Hotel to the Hotel Astoria, which was of much higher quality. The immigration authorities recognized Joe's proficiency in English and asked him to serve as a translator for the hundreds of newly arrived Czechoslovakian immigrants. Canada was very generous to us: we got free accommodations and a daily food allowance. Many of the immigrants in Ontario also received financial support for six months of full-time English-language instruction. After three days of working for them as a translator, the immigration officials sent Joe to the city hall building department to apply for a position as a civil engineer. His interview went well and he was offered a job that started within the week.

Gordon Singer, who was very successful – he had his own company, a private yacht and a beautiful house – advised Joe not to take the government job, but rather to look for a job with a private builder who would also give him a company car. Gordon offered to drive him to the various appointments that he had set up ahead of time. Within that first week, Joe was offered positions with five different companies. After consulting with Gordon, he decided to accept a position with H & R Developments (Hofstedter and Rubinstein), where he worked for seventeen years.

Now that Joe had a job, we rented a two-bedroom apartment in Leaside, at 892 Eglinton Avenue East. We chose that area on Aranka's suggestion, but although the apartment was much nicer than the place we had had in Košice, the superintendent turned out to be an antisemite. The Veselys had moved into the same building and none of us liked living there. Enrolling Tom and Katka in Leaside High School ended up being another bad decision. In hindsight, we realized that we should have moved to a Jewish area where the children would have been far more understanding of new immigrant children than was the case in the very settled Anglo-Saxon culture of Leaside.

Tom's experience at Leaside High School had a negative impact on him for many years. He started getting homesick and had trouble finding his place in this new society. Katka's situation was slightly better since she was able to make friends with two girls from immigrant families – Yuko Watanabe, a Japanese girl, and Jenin, an Arab girl. Although several other Czechoslovakian immigrant children attended the same school, both Tom and Katka still felt isolated and not at all accepted by most of their fellow students. After living in our apartment at 892 Eglinton Avenue East for five months, we decided to move to Thorncliffe Park, where a new Czechoslovakian community was developing.[1]

Unlike many other immigrants, I wasn't eligible for government-sponsored English-language training – only primary family earners who didn't have work were eligible and Joe had started working right away – so Agi Vesely and I started attending the International English Language Institute. I found it very arduous because learning new languages didn't come very easily to me. Nevertheless, I pushed myself hard as I desperately wanted to start working.

After seven months, I was offered a well-paying summer job as a nurse in the Agudah religious camp in Port Carling.[2] Another benefit was that I was also permitted to take Katka with me. When I arrived at the camp, I had to report to three rabbis from the United States and when I entered the room, I tried to shake their hands. Of course, they refused, which I couldn't understand.[3] They expressed disapproval and began speaking in Yiddish, which I also didn't understand. The rabbis complained that they had been promised a Jewish nurse and that there must have been some mistake because I didn't look Jewish, I didn't speak Yiddish and I had tried to shake their hands.

These issues got somewhat resolved when Joe came for a visit the next Sunday and, since his English was better than mine, explained to them that I was Jewish but had not been brought up in a religious environment. He also told them that not all Jews in Czechoslovakia speak Yiddish, so they agreed to let me and Katka stay for the rest of

---

1 Thorncliffe Park is a multicultural neighbourhood of Toronto that has been home to many immigrants. It is located in the east-central part of the city by the Don River.

2 Agudah camps are affiliated with Agudath Israel of America, an ultra-Orthodox Jewish organization with a network of social programs.

3 Rabbinic law prohibits unmarried members of the opposite sex to touch in any way, so strict observance would forbid a man to shake the hand of a woman who is not his wife.

the summer. The work wasn't easy – many of the kids were spoiled and I really struggled with my English – but Katka helped me with my shortcomings. I had a good knowledge of nursing and, all in all, the rabbis were satisfied with my performance. Katka made a lot of friends and, I think, had a pleasant summer, so my first job in Canada was quite a success.

After this summer job, I started looking for permanent work. The first place I turned to was the College of Nurses of Ontario, where I presented my documents, which had been translated from Slovak to English. Since I had a high school diploma and had graduated from two years of nursing education with honours, I was accepted right away. Nonetheless, my decision to enroll in the College of Nurses didn't have the outcome that I was hoping for – in Canada, my credentials restricted me to work in nursing homes or hospitals for physically disabled children. My only other option was to study for two more years to meet the Canadian requirements for a registered nurse.

After visiting a few of the institutions I was eligible to work in, I concluded that working in them would be too depressing for me and I would have to find another line of work. With my limited English, my choices were to work in a bank or an insurance company, where I would be dealing mainly with numbers. There was an insurance company called Wausau that was in the same building where Joe worked. The company had a job opening, so Joe made an appointment for me immediately. I was concerned about how I would do on the hiring test and whether I would be able to understand the questions. Joe was very encouraging, saying that it would likely be a simple mathematical test and numbers were the same in any language. He told me that if they asked me when I wanted to start, I should say, "As soon as possible." This I memorized and was hired within a few days. We started to feel more comfortable now that we both had steady jobs.

I started working at Wausau in September 1969 and was able to get a ride back and forth to work in Joe's company car. The president of the company, Mr. Ben Harrison, was wonderful to work for. A few months after I began work, there was a meeting to discuss hiring employees' children for summer jobs – there were seventy employees and only three positions, which were just being offered to girls. I didn't even bother applying because I was so happy just to have a job for myself. To my surprise, Mr. Harrison called me into his office and asked why I hadn't applied for any of the summer jobs for my daughter. When I told him the answer, he immediately filled in an application for Katka – now called Kathy – and the next day she was offered a job that would start after the school year ended. For the next four years, Kathy worked with me during all her school breaks. That first summer wasn't that lucrative for her, though. She worked in the mail department, where she had access to a phone and thought that all the calls were free. She spent hours talking on the telephone with her friend from Winnipeg, Eva Grunspan, and at the end of the summer, we were presented with a telephone bill that was almost equivalent to her summer earnings.

The only negative thing that happened in this period was that two years after we arrived in Canada, Ivan failed the Canadian dental certification examination. As a result, Hedi unfortunately convinced him to move to Israel, where his Czechoslovakian dental diploma would be recognized. It was an emotional farewell that I have never gotten over.

The same year that Ivan and Hedi moved to Israel – as soon as we could afford it – we brought my father and his wife from Košice to stay with us for six months. The airplane tickets were expensive and we also had to pay a substantial amount for medical insurance because of my father's heart problems and his wife's Parkinson's disease. They were our first visitors from Czechoslovakia – it was exciting not only for me, but also for many of my friends. The emotion of seeing my father arrive at the Toronto airport was indescribable. We gave my father and stepmother Tom's room in our three-bedroom apartment, and Tom slept in the living room. We had also recently taken in my sister-in-law's cousin from Israel, Gabi Spiegel – he was nineteen and, because of his poor health, his mother wanted him to avoid Israel's mandatory army draft. Gabi, who had just undergone an operation, was also sleeping in the living room. At the same time, Ivan came from Israel to see his parents, but only stayed for three weeks – he had recently suffered a mild heart attack and hadn't fully recovered. We had to borrow a bed from our friend Lilly Novak, and three people – Tom, Gabi and Ivan – all ended up having to sleep in the living room. Despite how crowded we were, I was so happy to have my father with me.

On the day my father arrived, at the very moment that we walked into our apartment from the airport, the telephone rang. I answered it and heard a woman's voice with a very heavy Hungarian accent on the other end. When I told her that she could speak to me in Hungarian, she said that she knew my aunt Ilonka from Los Angeles and was calling to send her love to me. She also explained that she was asking as many recent immigrants from Czechoslovakia as possible if they knew a man by the name of Edmund Grossmann. She didn't know if he had survived the war – nobody that she had talked to had any information about him. I told her that, as it happened, he was my father and, ironically, had just that very moment arrived from Košice. I explained that he had changed his name after the war and now went by the name Gonda, which was why no one knew what had happened to him. She was very excited and asked to speak to him; they talked for a long time. It turned out that this woman, Mrs. Muller, had been in love with my father many years before, and after she married, she and her husband had spent a great deal of time with my father and his wife.

Much as I loved having my father with me, it wasn't easy. He and my stepmother were used to having their main meal at noon, so I had to prepare food in the evenings for them to eat the next day. We would then eat the same food for our evening meal after work, and then, after dinner, I would cook the next day's meals. To make my life even more difficult, Gabi told Kathy and Tom that my stepmother was tasting the food straight from the pot, so Tom, Kathy and Gabi refused to eat from the same pot. I had to cook separate meals for them and for us. Fortunately, Kathy was very helpful – since she finished school two hours before we came home from work, she would call me and I would tell her over the phone how to prepare dinner. By the time we got home, Kathy would have an excellent dinner waiting for us. She was a tremendous help to me.

The six months of my father and stepmother's visit passed very quickly. I really wasn't looking forward to their departure. My father, by nature a fatalist, said that if it was in the cards for us to meet again, then it would happen – there was nothing I could do about it. I wish that I had inherited his nature. We tried to extend his stay, but the pension rules in Czechoslovakia were such that they would lose six months of their pension if they stayed any longer. After we got home from taking them to the airport, I felt empty and our apartment felt big and lonely.

Our lives went on. We both worked hard but were still very careful with our money. Instead of going to a hairdresser, for example, we bought a second-hand hairdryer and Kathy would regularly do our hair. My hair was very curly, though, so she had a hard time fixing it. On her way back from school one day, she stopped off at the shopping plaza at Thorncliffe Park and found a liquid for straightening curly hair. She told me about her discovery as soon as I got home from work and we went to the store and bought some. We read the instructions and she followed them step by step. At the end of the procedure, following the directions, she washed my hair, put it into rollers and turned on the hairdryer. I was watching TV and after a while I touched the rollers to see if my hair was dry. To my horror, my hair came off in my hand, still wrapped around the roller. I had gone completely bald! I was hysterical. I couldn't imagine how I could possibly go to work the next day. Kathy began to cry as well. With Joe, we went back to the store that had sold us the product and they contacted the manufacturer. He also bought me a wig.

I didn't go to work the next day. I went to the dermatologist, who assured me that my hair would grow back in a few months. The day after my appointment, an insurance representative from the manufacturer came to our house. When he asked me whether we had tested the product on a small area, instead of answering yes, I said no. Needless to say, we weren't compensated. I felt very uncomfortable with the way I looked in the wig. Everyone in my office was wondering what was going on. My hair started to grow back after three months and I started to regain my confidence. I still had to wear the wig for another seven months, though.

Now that we were more settled, Joe thought that it was time for us to buy a house. I wasn't very enthusiastic about the idea, but I eventually gave up opposing it. We bought a house with a huge, beautiful garden at 9 Chelford Road in Don Mills in December 1972 and moved in on May 25, 1973, Joe's fifty-third birthday. Our house became a meeting place for Czech and Slovak expatriates for twenty-five years and I organized lots of garden parties there – some of them for more than sixty people.

Our children's lives were changing as well. After Tom completed high school in 1971, he was accepted to the University of Toronto, to the physical education program. We weren't enthusiastic about his choice and we recognized that, all in all, he wasn't happy in Canada. So we weren't surprised when, after almost completing one year of university, he decided to immigrate to Israel and study at the renowned Wingate Institute for Physical Education. It was very difficult for me to see him go. However, he wasn't pleased with this career choice either and came back to Toronto in the fall of 1973 to study dentistry at George Brown, following in both his grandfather's and uncle's footsteps.

Kathy was also undergoing quite a few changes – she had developed into a beautiful young girl and lots of the Czechoslovakian boys had more than a mild interest in her. She had started a relationship with one of them, a boy named Michal whose parents were friends of ours. Their romance lasted for almost three years, until Kathy finished high school. After her graduation in 1973 we sent her to Israel for the summer before starting university – she had already been accepted to the University of Toronto. We advised Kathy to meet other boys and we gave Michal the same advice about meeting other girls. I told Kathy that she had yet to meet the man who would become her prince. Of course she didn't believe me at the time, but, as always, I followed my instincts.

In the summer of 1973, both Kathy and Tom were in Israel, and we were very lonely in our castle, our first home. Not only were both our children away, but our beautiful Husky dog named Bonzo ran away too. Joe's view was that we should take more time for ourselves now, take life a little easier. He didn't think that I should be in the office every day from morning until late in the evening and suggested that I enroll in a real estate course. I could still keep my job while I was working toward my real estate license, but once I finished the course, I could leave the insurance company.

I enjoyed my work at the insurance company. When my supervisor was fired, I took over her functions. I did the work of the supervisor for several months and I got a salary increase, but I wasn't officially given the job. One day, however, there was an announcement that another person had been named supervisor instead of me. I was so infuriated that I walked out. I called Joe and told him that I had just quit my job. He thought that I was overreacting and tried to talk me out of quitting. After all, he said, the company wasn't cutting my salary.

I stayed home the next day and, to my surprise, a whole delegation from my office showed up and tried to convince me to come back to work. They insisted that the decision had not been a reflection on the quality of my work, but that the woman who was appointed supervisor had seniority over me and spoke better English. I went back to the office with them and called Joe, who was very pleased with my decision.

Despite my decision to go back to work at Wausau, in January 1974 I followed Joe's suggestion and enrolled in a four-month evening real estate course. I successfully finished the course and gave notice at work. Not only did they try to talk me out of my decision, but they also arranged a beautiful goodbye party with a special gift. I was also presented with a letter from Ben Harrison, the company president, stating that I could return to work at any time, that they would always accept me back. I treasure that letter to this day.

On October 19, 1974, I was very excited because my first house sale was to be concluded that evening. My good friend Laci Kivovic was helpful and explained to me that I had the wrong approach to selling a house. I shouldn't concern myself with how the client would be able to pay, but instead should focus on selling the property. He promised to help me with the presentation at seven o'clock that evening.

That same day, Joe called to ask me to meet him at a travel agency in Thorncliffe Plaza at five o'clock to plan our first vacation since moving to Canada. On the way to the travel agency, I stopped at McDonald's to get a hamburger and arrived at the plaza just before five. I was wearing very high heels and while I was running down the stairs, I slipped on a plum skin and broke my ankle so badly that I could hear my bones crack. I was in terrible pain but got up and then fell again, making the pain even worse. A few moments later, Joe arrived to find me on the stairs, surrounded by a lot of people. The security guard had called an ambulance as I lay on the floor. I tried to convince everybody that I had to get to my appointment, but the ambulance took me to East York General Hospital instead.

I was sure that the doctors would put on a cast and let me leave so that I could make it to my seven o'clock presentation on time. After the X-ray, however, they called Joe in and told us that I had a very serious fracture and would have to undergo immediate surgery. Unfortunately, because I had just eaten the hamburger, the surgery had to be postponed until the next day.

I phoned the children to let them know what had happened and then had to call Laci Kivovic and ask him to represent me at the house appointment. The nurses took me to a hospital room and tried to ease my pain. The next day I underwent major surgery for three and a half hours. The surgeon, Dr. Evans, had to put a number of screws and metal plates in my leg to fix my ankle. When I came out of the anesthetic, Dr. Evans was beside my bed, telling me about my condition – it sounded very serious. He told me that some of the metal inserts would most likely have to stay inside my ankle permanently. That really frightened me. I was forty-four years old and I knew that I would have to work until I reached retirement age – another twenty-one years.

I was really worried that I would have a permanent limp, but I didn't know how to say "limp" in English so I asked Dr. Evans whether I would be able to ski and skate, which made me sound like an Olympic champion. He said noncommittally, "We'll see how your healing progresses." A little while later, an attractive young doctor, Dr. Steven Samuel, came into the room to take care of another patient and asked me what language I spoke. He said that he could help translate for me if I spoke either Hebrew or Hungarian. I was very relieved and explained to him in Hungarian that I had only asked Dr. Evans about skiing and skating because I didn't know the proper word in English. He was very supportive and helpful.

I was in the hospital for nine days. Kathy visited me every day and I began to have a feeling that she and Dr. Samuel were interested in each other. I came right out and asked the doctor if he was still single. He was. Before I left the hospital, I gave him my real estate agent card. I knew that Kathy still had feelings for Michal, but I was secretly hoping that a romance would develop between my daughter and Steve Samuel. After I got home from the hospital, he called me and asked how I was. It was funny because he mixed up our names, calling me Kathy and asking me where Agi was. That was the beginning of their close relationship.

One day, Steve Samuel invited us to a concert at the University of Toronto. Ironically, he was playing the first violin and beside him was Michal, playing the second violin. Lilly Novak was with us and predicted that from now on, Michal would always play second fiddle in Kathy's life. Nine months into Steve and Kathy's relationship, on August 13, 1975, in our garden at 9 Chelford Road, Steve asked our permission to marry Kathy. It was one of the happiest days of my life. I had been fond of Steve from the first moment I met him and had a mother's intuition that Kathy would be well cared for in the future.

After receiving our blessing, Steve called his parents, Ocsi and Anyuci, to come over to share the good news with all of us. When they arrived less than half an hour later, Ocsi was carrying Anyuci in his arms. We were concerned, but Ocsi told us that Anyuci often collapsed when she got very excited and simply couldn't walk right then. Steve's parents were as thrilled as Joe and I were. We had a very close relationship as in-laws that everyone admired. We sat together in the garden that first day and began to plan our children's wedding for June 1, 1976. Anyuci organized an engagement party in their party room with approximately thirty guests. We gradually met the whole Samuel family, including his brother Oded, who had been at the University of Toronto with Kathy.

About a month before the wedding, I underwent another operation to remove all of the hardware from my ankle. The doctor hadn't counted on such a positive outcome and was extremely pleased; the healing had happened much faster than expected because I was still young and very healthy. Since my real estate career had never really been able to get off the ground, I returned to the insurance company, where I was welcomed back with open arms.

Anyuci and I threw ourselves into the big preparations for the wedding. We sent Ivan an airplane ticket for the wedding, but he and his family regrettably couldn't attend because my father and his wife had gone to visit him in Israel and they had to take care of my stepmother, who now had advanced Parkinson's. My father arrived in Toronto three days before the wedding, though, and seeing him again was an absolute joy for me.

The wedding took place at Shaarei Shomayim synagogue. The bride and groom were such beautiful young people and Ocsi used to say that it was the wedding of the century. Sitting at the head table from our family were Joe and I, my father, Tom, Aunt Aranka and Uncle Fred, Joe's brother Robert, my mother's cousin Ilonka and Joe's cousin Otto from Germany. The Samuel family was represented by Anyuci and Ocsi, Ocsi's sister, Rachi, and her husband, Albert, Anyuci's aunt Edith and sister Honorka, her husband, Shalom, and Oded, Steve's brother and best man.

The speeches were memorable and hilarious – Ocsi's was the most unforgettable and the most sentimental. Everything, unfortunately, must come to an end. Kathy and Steve left at midnight and an hour or two after that the wedding was over. I found myself looking for Kathy before we left and felt empty inside knowing that I would be going home without her. Our house was full of guests, though. Staying with us were my father, cousin Otto, my old and dear friend Magda and her mother, Julish. Still, the house felt empty without Kathy. My father left for Israel on June 15, the day before my birthday, and Tom left for Israel three days later. He had already finished George Brown College with the idea of settling permanently in Israel and working as a dental technician.

I now had a completely empty nest. Even though I was working full-time, my life changed dramatically. For a long time I couldn't accept the fact that Kathy's focus would now be on her new husband. I needlessly gave her a hard time because of the emotional turmoil that I was going through. Unlike Joe, who was preoccupied with his work, I couldn't stand the silence in the house. Following someone's advice, I turned to yoga and meditation.

Life went on and I slowly started to accept things as they were. We were in regular touch with Tom. At one point he complained that he had a urinary infection that wasn't being looked after properly in Israel and was thinking of returning to Canada for treatment. I opposed the idea simply because I couldn't bear the thought of having him home with us only to say goodbye yet again. Joe, however, advised me to encourage Tom to come. I gave in, thinking that perhaps I could convince him to stay in Canada. Fortunately, my plan worked, and in June 1977 Tom got an excellent job teaching dentistry at the University of Toronto, where he still works more than twenty-five years later.

Joe and I both continued to work very hard – I was still working in the credit department at the insurance company – but now that we were on our own we started to take wonderful holidays. Most of them were in the winter with our friends, but we also travelled to Israel almost every year because Ivan's health was deteriorating – he had had his first heart attack at the age of thirty-six.

In January 1978, we went on a beautiful holiday in Hawaii with our friends Imre and Magda Reitmann. Imre happened to remark in passing that his friend Paul Rigor, who owned a restaurant and bakery called Cake Master, was looking for someone reliable to work for him as a sales manager and would double my salary. I jumped at the opportunity even though it wasn't easy leaving the insurance company again. They organized another party for mc with beautiful presents and hoped that I would come back one day.

I really loved my new job, not only because of my excellent salary but also because I got a chance to meet such famous people as Adrienne Clarkson, governor general of Canada; Barbara Amiel, the wife of Conrad Black; Barbara's ex-husband, well-known Hungarian-born Canadian writer George Jonas; acclaimed architect Sidney Bregman; the Roman family, owners of Denison mines; and the famous lawyer Edward Greenspan and his wife, Suzy.

My life was now taking a turn for the better, particularly after Kathy announced that we were going to be grandparents. The day that my first grandchild was born, August 30, 1978, I rushed to Mount Sinai hospital, where the whole family and a few of Kathy's friends had gathered. We were a boisterous crowd and the hospital staff kept warning us over the intercom that we would have to leave the waiting room if we didn't quiet down. The magnificent moment finally arrived when Steve came out of the delivery room with a beautiful little girl who introduced herself by looking at each of us one by one (although I'm sure that she looked at me the longest, telling me, "Babi, I am Daniella"). Tears of joy rolled down my face. I had become a grandmother at the age of forty-eight – it was one of the most precious gifts that Kathy could have given me. Joe and I visited our beautiful granddaughter every day after work.

Kathy had graduated from the University of Toronto with an honours Bachelor of Science degree in medical microbiology in June 1977. The next year, on June 16, 1978, she graduated from the same university's faculty of education, just two months before Daniella was born. That December, Joe and I decided to send Kathy and Steve to Hawaii as a reward for working so hard. We stayed with Daniella, who was four months old at the time. Before Kathy and Steve left on their holiday, I bought a long, dark wig because Daniella liked to play with her mother's long hair while she nursed and I wanted to make the separation of mother and daughter easier. My ruse worked – Daniella seemed to think that I was her mother as she played with the wig while I fed her.

As the months elapsed, Daniella developed into a beautiful young toddler. When she was ten months old, Kathy announced to us that we were going to be grandparents for a second time. Again, we were thrilled. I had always dreamt of having lots of children, but my life in Czechoslovakia had been too complicated. I was glad that Kathy would now fulfil my dreams.

It was around this time that my uncle Sanyi came for a visit after going to see his daughter, Katka, and her family in Washington, DC. He was eighty-five years old and in excellent physical and mental condition, but he only knew how to speak one language, Hungarian. Although he had lived in Košice for eighteen years, he couldn't speak a word of Slovak. A funny situation occurred as a result. Katka had arranged for him to be transported by wheelchair in order to minimize his language problems. When he arrived at the Washington airport and was taken to customs, the official started to speak to him in English, which of course he didn't understand. The customs officer then looked at his passport and saw that he was from Czechoslovakia, so he arranged to bring in a Slovak translator who began talking to him in Slovak. Again, he couldn't understand what anyone was saying and the officials came to the conclusion that he must have brain damage. They finally located Katka through the paging system and she was able to help bridge the communication barrier.

While he was in Toronto Uncle Sanyi visited Kathy several times and nicknamed Daniella "Shirley Temple." I found out later that he had secretly asked Joe to take him to a pornographic movie because such things didn't exist where he came from. Joe had never been to that kind of place, but of course he went with Uncle Sanyi anyway. They had a great time and I wasn't supposed to know anything about it. We were all very sad when Uncle Sanyi left Toronto – we didn't know if we would ever meet again.

The months passed and on March 9, 1980, our grandson Jonathan was born. We gathered again in the same hospital – Mount Sinai – and after several hours of waiting, Steve came out of the delivery room to announce that he had a son. We were all delighted, especially the Samuels, because having a boy was very important to them. Our two families arranged a nice bris at the hospital.[4] Daniella, who was not quite two, was a bit disoriented by the new situation, and a bit jealous. We made sure to pay lots of attention to her and it wasn't long before the two children were playing together in the same crib. It was so wonderful to see our two gorgeous grandchildren side by side.

---

4 A bris is a Jewish religious ceremony to welcome male infants into the covenant with God. It involves ritual circumcision and is performed eight days after the baby is born. For more information, see the glossary.

More Endings and More Beginnings

We had already made plans for a trip to Israel at the end of October 1980 when Joe got an invitation to visit Robert and his family in Athens and see the Greek islands. He was excited to find out that we could stop over in Athens without paying any more for the flight. But I experienced one of my strong premonitions and told him, "You go to Athens – I'm going to Budapest to see my father." I couldn't risk going to Košice – we weren't actually allowed to go into Czechoslovakia at all because the Communists were still very much in control of the country and we were considered to be defectors. According to Czech law, if we were caught inside the country, we would be sentenced to a long jail term. I told Joe that I needed to see my father as soon as possible – I sensed that this would likely be my last chance to see him. The Greek islands would be there in the future. He understood how I felt and instead of going to Greece, we both arranged to stop off in Budapest to visit our cousins Heda and Pista, and have my father meet us there.

On the day before our departure we were told that we needed visas with our photos on them to enter Hungary. We didn't have much time, so we took pictures of ourselves in a photo booth and hurried to the Hungarian consulate to get our documents. We went to Israel for ten days and had a wonderful time. We were still concerned about going even close to our homeland – we hadn't been back for twelve years. Even going to Budapest was a risk; we were worried that we might even be extradited from Hungary to Czechoslovakia.

When we landed in Budapest and got into the passport lineup, we saw a lot of uniformed men carrying guns walking around. People in Toronto had told us not to let the customs officers know that we understood Hungarian. Joe was in front of me at the passport control and it took a long time for him to get processed, but they let him through. Then it was my turn. The customs officers asked me if I spoke Hungarian and I said no. When they looked at my visa, they objected to my photo, insisting that it didn't look like me. I was starting to get frightened – my passport showed that I was born in Czechoslovakia.

The officers decided to call their superior and when he arrived and looked at my documents, he also said, "This isn't you." He decided to compare my signature to the one on my passport and visa. They handed me a pen and asked me to sign a paper. I was so scared that my hands were shaking, so my signature didn't look anything like the one on my passport. I was so shaken that I forgot that I had told them that I couldn't speak Hungarian and said, in Hungarian, "Please call my husband to help me out." The passport officer asked, "Madame, why didn't you speak Hungarian from the beginning?" By the time they brought Joe I was almost in tears. Whatever he said to them satisfied their questions and they let me go. Our five-day adventure in Hungary had a terrifying beginning.

Once we had cleared customs, we were greeted by Heda and Pista who had been waiting for us at the airport. They took us to their apartment, which was quite large. Uncle Sanyi had accompanied my father from Košice and we had a joyous reunion with him. Unfortunately, though, my father was in poor psychological shape – he had always been full of energy and good humour, but now he wasn't interested in anything. He told me that my stepmother's condition had deteriorated so much that he had to take complete care of her, which was taking a terrible toll on him. During our five-day stay, we spent all our time with him and Uncle Sanyi, who was now a widower. Aunt Lotte had passed away shortly after his return from his visit to North America, but he was in much better shape than my father.

We notified the Canadian embassy that we were in Budapest – since we were travelling as Canadian citizens, they could help us if we were arrested while we were in Hungary. Our five days passed much too quickly. We told my father that if my stepmother passed away, he shouldn't worry about anything. We would send him an airplane ticket right away and he could live with us.

On the fifth day of our stay in Budapest, Joe and I had a flight to Toronto in the afternoon, and my father and uncle had railway tickets to Košice that same morning. I couldn't sleep all night, certain that this was the last time I would see my father and my uncle. My cousins, Pista, Heda, her husband, Pali, and Eva and Joe and I all went to the railway station in the morning to say goodbye to them. We stood under the train window, holding their hands. When the train started to pull away from the station, I said to my cousins, "This is my last meeting with my father and my uncle; we will never see them again."

To this day, my cousins from Budapest are struck by my foresight. About three weeks after we came home, on December 8, 1980, my father suddenly passed away while watching television. My stepmother was bedridden and didn't know what had happened. He was found the next day, still sitting in his armchair, holding a piece of bread. When my relatives called to tell me about his death, I was devastated. I was now an orphan.

Joe began making arrangements for my trip to the funeral in Košice. I already had my airplane ticket, but my visa required approval from the Czechoslovakian consulate. Since the Communist regime still considered me to be a defector, however, the consulate flatly refused to give me permission even after several phone calls begging them to let me go to my father's funeral. The consular authorities told Joe, "We have no sympathy for people who escaped from Czechoslovakia illegally." Joe replied, "I know you aren't sympathetic, but you're also not humane."

Israel didn't have diplomatic relations with Czechoslovakia, so Ivan wasn't able to go to Košice for the funeral either. Had we risked going, we likely would have been incarcerated for many years. So my beloved father was buried without the presence of either of his two children. I sat shiva at our house in Toronto.[1] My pain at losing my father and not being able to be with family in Czechoslovakia was almost unbearable.

Although my stepmother had never treated me well, we supported her financially after my father's death. We were concerned about the quality of her life in Czechoslovakia and tried to bring her to Toronto, but with the kind of illness she had, the immigration department refused to accept her into Canada. She died on November 24, 1981, just eleven months after my father. Uncle Sanyi died three months later on March 12, 1982, at the age of eighty-seven. One year later, just as my uncle Jozko was preparing to come for a visit to Canada, he passed away in Bratislava. A few years later, I also lost my uncle Ruven, who died in Israel on Kibbutz Ma'anit. This generation of my family was no more.

Life went on and, after so many deaths in the family, the birth of our third grandchild, Michelle, on March 12, 1982, was a particular blessing. Our good fortune continued when two years later our fourth grandchild, Elliott, came into the world on June 21, 1984. Now much of our free time was spent with Kathy and our grandchildren.

In 1985, Ivan had to undergo bypass surgery in Israel. It was a risky procedure, so instead of taking a vacation that year, I went to Israel to be with my brother and Hedika, for moral support. It was August and the heat in Israel was stifling. I was only able to stay for a few days after Ivan was discharged from the hospital because I had to go back to work. I would have liked to stay longer and it was very hard to leave Ivan. We all cried when it was time for me to leave for the airport.

---

1   In Judaism, shiva (meaning "seven" in Hebrew) is the seven-day mourning period that is observed after the funeral of a close relative.

Not long after I returned home from Israel, Joe decided, at the age of sixty-six, to accept a new job instead of retiring. He went to work at the Conservatory Group, building condominiums and townhouses. Along with his new work, he undertook the building of a second-storey addition to Kathy's house and the reconstruction of a rental building for Tom. I tried to warn him to slow down, but he wouldn't listen. I told him something bad would happen and unfortunately I was right. On December 10, 1987, Joe had a heart attack. He was discharged from the hospital three weeks later with the following warning from his doctor, "Mr. Tomasov, you should consider your-self lucky. You suffered a massive heart attack, however, I believe that you will be able to live a normal life. Until now you've been driving a six-cylinder car. From now on, your capacity is like a two-cylinder car. You must learn to live according to this limitation, slow down and change your lifestyle."

After he came home from the hospital, Joe was so weak that he couldn't even walk around the dining table. It wasn't easy for us all to see such a drastic change in him. He went from being a hyperactive person to a dependent one. During the three months that he needed intensive home care, I tried my very best to be patient and boost Joe's confidence, and provide him with the highest standard of care. I gave him vitamins and cooked him food according to the Heart and Stroke Foundation of Canada's guidelines. His health improved slowly and in March 1988, he returned to work part-time. He also participated in a rehabilitation program and began to exercise on a regular basis, walking every day. This helped him become much more optimistic about his future.

During October of that year, we went on vacation to a Budapest thermal spa for two weeks with Anyuci and Ocsi. On the fifth day of our vacation, I received a phone call from cousin Heda telling me that Ivanko had died of his fourth heart attack. The pain I felt was so deep, it was as if part of my body and soul had been amputated. To this day, I feel a terrible void in my life – I will never get over losing my brother. The next day, I flew to Israel to be at his funeral. I asked Anyuci to take care of Joe and watch over his medication until my return. My flight to Israel was incredibly sad, knowing that my brother wouldn't be waiting for me at the airport as he had done so many times in the past. With Ivan's death, another important chapter of my life closed.

When I arrived at their house, I found Hedika with Ivetka and her two small children. Hedika was in desperate shape. The funeral of my little brother, Ivanko, took place the next day. I have blocked the details from my memory. We sat shiva and meanwhile, Kathy sent a return airplane ticket for Hedika to come to Canada and spend the winter with us. Before I left, I went to the cemetery to say goodbye to Ivanko and promised him that I would take care of his wife. It was only possible for me to leave Israel because I knew Hedika would be with us again soon.

Hedika did come and spend the winter with us, but she was very depressed. We tried our best to give her love and confidence and I assured her that I would never abandon her. For the first several days of her stay, she had horrible nightmares. I asked Joe to switch rooms with her so that she could sleep with me in our bedroom, where I could hold her hands and calm her down. She was shaking and sweating most of the time, but after a couple of weeks she started to feel better and told me that she felt that she was strong enough to sleep alone in her room.

After five months with us, just before Passover, Hedika decided that she felt strong enough to return to Israel.[2] She felt that she had left Ivetka alone long enough. But only a few days after settling back in Israel, she told me that she missed my strength and encouragement. We decided that she would return to Canada after the high holidays (Rosh Hashanah and Yom Kippur) the following year and

_____

2   For more information on the significant Jewish holidays of Passover, Rosh Hashanah and Yom Kippur, see the glossary.

spend the winter with us again. We sent her the airline ticket right away, so she would feel secure and know that she was welcome.

Hedika came back to Canada the next fall. This visit was easier for all of us because, with the passage of time, her depression had lessened. I came to the conclusion that as painful as it would be for me, I should encourage her to get married again. She was still relatively young, only forty-nine, and because of Ivan's long illness, she was not financially secure. After her second winter in Canada, Hedika returned back home before Pesach 1991.

That summer, now that the Communist regime had fallen, Joe and I decided to go to Czechoslovakia to visit the graves of our beloved parents.[3] We called my cousins Heda and Pali in Budapest to let them know that we were coming. They were delighted to hear it and picked us up at the airport and took us to their place. They had a big apartment in the heart of Budapest. When we arrived, they introduced us to a friend of theirs from Israel, Tibi Cohen. I asked him bluntly where his wife was and he answered that he had been divorced for ten years. He was attractive and approximately my age, so it struck me that he could be a good match for Hedika. I told him that I had a beautiful sister-in-law in Israel and he replied that he had no intention of getting married again. The next day, however, I bought a Hungarian cosmetic cream and I asked him to please take it to Hedika when he returned to Israel. I was positive that he would like her. I wasn't wrong – after several months, sure enough, they got married. He had a beautiful apartment in Haifa and is not only a loving husband to Hedika, but also a devoted grandfather to her grandchildren.

---

3   In November 1989, student and worker protests against communism in Prague quickly gained momentum throughout the country, a period known as the Velvet Revolution (in Slovakia it is known as the Gentle Revolution). In the face of mounting pressure, the Communist regime resigned on November 28. A non-Communist government was appointed on December 10 and in June 1990 Czechoslovakia held the first democratic elections in over forty years.

Next it was Tom's turn. He decided to visit Prague and Košice in the hopes that he would find somebody to share his future with. Fate was good to him too. He met a girl named Janka Hrusovska in Košice and after several weeks, Janka came to Toronto for a visit. The two of them became closer and they decided to get married. We were overjoyed to welcome Janka into our family. We arranged the wedding for May 6, 1994, and held a reception for fifty-eight guests at our house at 9 Chelford Road. Janka was very pleased with how easily we accepted her. She wrote in a letter to her parents that she felt I didn't deserve to be called mother-in-law because I treated her like a daughter. I was very pleased to hear that from her mother, Marika, as I too felt that Janka was like a second daughter to me.

Following this happy occasion, we were blessed with two more wonderful and beautiful grandchildren, Nicole who was born on February 12, 1995, and our youngest grandson, Matthew, who was born on November 16, 1997. We are the grandparents of the six most amazing grandchildren in the whole world (not that I'm biased).

In 1998, after a long-running disagreement with Joe, we sold our house at 9 Chelford Road – he was reluctant to leave the house where we had lived for twenty-five years, but he finally gave in and we purchased a beautiful condominium that he renovated. The building has indoor and outdoor swimming pools, five tennis courts, a gym and many cultural programs that we participate in. We hope that we will be healthy and live in it for many years to come. We are surrounded by many of our best friends, which makes our life even more enjoyable.

Time has gone by unbelievably fast. Our four eldest grandchildren have already had beautiful bar and bat mitzvahs. With so much family around us, our life has been more hopeful and happier than I ever thought it would be.

Epilogue

Joe and I now had a beautiful family and a community of close friends and we continued to work full-time. Despite our hectic schedules, we were fortunate to be able to travel the world. We visited Israel nine times, including one trip with our eldest grandchild, Daniella. We toured all over Europe with organized excursions to Holland, Belgium, France, Luxembourg, Germany, Switzerland and Italy. Then we travelled extensively through Spain, Portugal and Morocco, where Tom joined us. We also went to Western Canada – the Rocky Mountains, Vancouver, Calgary and Victoria. We were able to take beautiful cruises to Alaska and the Caribbean. The most memorable cruise was one we took on Tom's fiftieth birthday – a Baltic cruise that began in London and then sailed from England to Denmark, Sweden, Finland, Saint Petersburg, Russia, and to Oslo, Norway and then back to London, where we stayed several days to explore that remarkable city.

A short time later, we went on a three-week cruise to South America, visiting the Iguassu Falls in Argentina, Brazil, the Falkland Islands, Uruguay, and Cape Horn and Santiago in Chile. Our next big adventure was a trip to the Fiji Islands, where we spent three days before travelling to New Zealand for nine days. In our opinion, although the Alps and the fjords were breathtaking, we considered New Zealand to be the most beautiful part of the world.

From New Zealand we flew to Australia, which had tremendous significance for us because we had almost immigrated there in 1949. In Melbourne, we met our friend Bandi Steiner, who had not only introduced me to Joe in Levice, but had also been one of the witnesses at our wedding. After forty-five years, this meeting was very emotional. We spent the next twelve days travelling around Australia, visiting Sydney, Melbourne, Adelaide, Brisbane, Cairns, the Great Barrier Reef and Ayers Rock. After seeing the sights in this magnificent part of the world, we flew to Hawaii for our third visit to those beautiful islands.

The following year, Joe persuaded me to visit the Far East. I found the trip interesting, but very tiring. We flew from Toronto to Alaska and from there to Hong Kong and Beijing. The flight took twenty-two hours. The next day our guide took us to Beijing to see examples of its incredibly old culture and two days later we went to the Great Wall. The day after that we were taken to the port city of Tientsin, where we boarded a cruise ship and sailed to Seoul in South Korea, and from there to Shanghai, Saigon in Vietnam, Malaysia, Kuala Lumpur and finally to Singapore and Bangkok, where we visited the beautiful pagodas. We took guided tours of all those wondrous cities. We left the cruise ship in Bangkok and flew to Hong Kong for more sightseeing and finally back to Toronto, where we arrived exhausted but enriched by our extraordinary experiences.

In addition to our world travels, we also made several more trips to our native country of Czechoslovakia since our first historic trip in 1991. On my seventieth birthday, June 16, 2000, I went to the cemetery to thank my mother and father for all my blessings.

My reason for describing all our travels in such detail and with such enthusiasm is that, for those of us who survived both the terrible years of Nazi persecution and the oppressive years of Communism, being able to see the world, to travel wherever we liked, was a dream come true.

∼

I cannot believe that almost fifty-five years have elapsed since fate joined my life to that of my dear husband, the father of my two beloved children and the grandfather of our six amazing grandchildren. We went through many hardships together but somehow, with God's help, we always managed to land on our feet. Neither of us had any help or guidance from our parents – perhaps that's why we cherish the successes that we have had. I'm closing my memoir today on December 1, 2003, with the following benediction to my husband, my children and my grandchildren:

> May the Lord bless you and guard you.
> May the Lord show you favour and be gracious to you.
> May the Lord show you kindness and grant you peace.

Glossary

aliyah (Hebrew; literally, "ascent"; pl. *aliyot*) A term used by Jews and modern Israelis to refer to Jewish immigration to Israel; the term is also used to refer to "going up" to the altar in a synagogue to read from the Torah.

antisemitism Prejudice, discrimination, persecution and/or hatred against Jewish people, institutions, culture and symbols.

Auschwitz (German; in Polish, Oświęcim) A town in southern Poland approximately thirty-seven kilometres from Krakow, it is also the name of the largest complex of Nazi concentration camps that were built nearby. The Auschwitz complex contained three main camps: Auschwitz I, a slave labour camp built in May 1940; Auschwitz-Birkenau, a death camp built in early 1942; and Auschwitz-Monowitz, a slave labour camp built in October 1942. In 1941, Auschwitz I was a testing site for usage of the lethal gas Zyklon B as a method of mass killing. The Auschwitz complex was liberated by the Soviet army in January 1945.

Ayers Rock Also known as Uluru, it is a large sandstone rock that is the remnant of an eroded mountain range in central Australia; it is a United Nations World Heritage Site.

bar mitzvah/bat mitzvah (Hebrew; literally, one to whom commandments apply) The age of thirteen when, according to Jewish tradition, boys become religiously and morally responsible for

their actions and are considered adults for the purpose of synagogue ritual. A bar mitzvah is also the synagogue ceremony and
family celebration that mark the attainment of this status, during
which the boy is called upon to read a portion of the Torah and
recite the prescribed prayers in a public prayer forum (minyan).
In the latter half of the twentieth century, liberal Jews instituted
an equivalent ceremony and celebration for girls – called a bat
mitzvah – which takes place at the age of twelve.

bris (Yiddish; in Hebrew, *brit milah*, literally meaning "covenant of
circumcision") Judaism's religious ceremony to welcome male infants into the covenant between God and the Children of Israel
through a ritual circumcision performed by a mohel, or circum-
ciser, eight days after the baby is born. Traditionally, a baby boy is
named after his bris.

chuppah (Hebrew; literally "covering" or "canopy") The canopy used
in traditional Jewish weddings, usually made of a cloth (sometimes a prayer shawl) stretched or supported over four poles. A
chuppah is meant to symbolize the home the couple will build
together.

Dubček, Alexander The Slovak politician who replaced Antonín
Novotný as First Secretary of the Communist Party on January
5, 1968, and implemented a program of liberal reforms known as
"The Prague Spring." The political and economic reforms implemented under Dubček's leadership resulted in greater freedom for
Czech citizens as he sought to replace the repressive, totalitarian
style of Communism with a more humane socialism. His April
1968 Action Program of democratic reforms included freedom
of the press, freedom of speech and assembly, and greater freedom to travel. During his regime, which only lasted from January
to August 1968, Dubček also federalized Czechoslovakia, creat-
ing the separate Czech Socialist Republic and Slovak Socialist
Republic. The latter change was the only Dubček reform to survive the end of the Prague Spring.

February 1948 Revolution The non-violent seizure of power by the Communist Party in Czechoslovakia led by Communist leader Klement Gottwald in February 1948. It effectively ended democratic governance in Czechoslovakia until 1990.

Hashomer Hatzair A left-wing Zionist youth movement founded in Central Europe in the early twentieth century to prepare young Jews to become workers and farmers, to establish kibbutzim – collective settlements – in pre-state Israel and work the land as pioneers. Before World War II, there were 70,000 Hashomer Hatzair members worldwide and many of them led resistance activities in the ghettos and concentration camps or joined partisan groups in the forests of east-central Europe. It is the oldest Zionist youth movement still in existence.

Hasidic Judaism (from the Hebrew word *hasid*, literally meaning "piety") A Jewish spiritual movement founded by Rabbi Israel ben Eliezer in eighteenth-century Poland; characterized by philosophies of mysticism and focusing on joyful prayer. There are many different sects of Hasidic Judaism, but followers of Hasidism often wear dark, conservative clothes as well as a head covering to reflect modesty and show respect to God.

Hebrew Immigrant Aid Society (HIAS) Founded in New York in 1881, the Hebrew Immigrant Aid Society provides aid, counsel, support and general assistance to Jewish immigrants all over the world. Since the early 1970s, HIAS has been especially active in providing assistance to Jews emigrating from the USSR.

Hlinka's Slovak People's Party (HSSP) Named for its founder and first chairman, Father Andrej Hlinka, the HSSP was a strongly nationalist, Catholic, totalitarian party that became the first government of the newly autonomous Slovakian Republic in 1939. Its wartime president, who had taken over as chairman of the HSSP after Hlinka's death in 1938, was Catholic priest Jozef Tiso. The Hlinka Guard, the paramilitary wing of the new autonomous Slovak regime, was established in October 1938.

Iron Curtain A term coined by Sir Winston Churchill in 1946 to describe the metaphorical boundary that physically and ideologically divided Europe into two separate spheres of influence at the end of World War II: one in Eastern Europe, controlled politically, militarily and economically by the Soviet Union; the second in Western Europe, allied with Western liberal democracies, economically predisposed to market economics and under the military protection of the United States.

kangaroo court Slang terminology for court proceedings that are either fixed or illegitimate; literally signifies courts taking "leaps" of justice. East European Communist governments were infamous for manipulating the judicial system.

Masaryk, Jan (1886–1948) The son of Tomas G. Masaryk, the founder and first president of Czechoslovakia. Educated in Czechoslovakia and the United States, Jan Masaryk served Czechoslovakia as ambassador to the United Kingdom until his country was overrun by the Germans in 1938. During World War II, Jan Masaryk served as foreign minister to the Czech government-in-exile, a position he retained in the provisional, multi-party National Front government established in Czechoslovakia following the liberation of his country from the Germans in 1945. In 1948, following a consolidation of a Communist, Soviet-led government, Jan Masaryk was found dead in his pyjamas in the courtyard of his apartment building. There was ongoing debate and investigations into whether he committed suicide, as was proclaimed by the Communist government, or whether he was thrown to his death by Communist thugs. A final investigation, concluded in December 2003, proved that Masaryk was murdered through the testimony of an expert witness who studied the position of the body when it was found. However, this new evidence did not lead to any prosecutions.

Masaryk, Tomas G. (1850–1937) Founder and first president of Czechoslovakia. He was known for his strong public opposition to antisemitism.

May Day Also known as International Workers' Day, May Day is celebrated on May 1 in many countries around the world in recognition of the achievements of workers and the international labour movement. It was first celebrated in Russia on May 1, 1917. In countries other than Canada and the United States – where Labour Day is considered the official holiday for workers – May Day is marked by huge street rallies led by workers, trade unions, anarchists and various communist and socialist parties.

May Tree In Slovak tradition, a tree, usually pine and decorated with ribbons, that is planted or placed by a boy in front of the house of the girl he is interested in. The custom is usually carried out on May 1, or May Day.

meningitis A potentially life-threatening illness that involves the inflammation of the membranes covering the brain and spinal cord (the meninges); symptoms include headache, fever and vomiting.

moshav (Hebrew; literally, "settlement" or "village") Founded by the left-wing Zionist youth movement, *moshava* camps simulated life on a kibbutz – a cooperative, communal farming community in Palestine – while teaching campers about Judaism and socialism.

Nováky The largest labour camp in Slovakia, it was divided into two sections – one was a labour camp and the other a transit camp, where prisoners were deported to death camps in Auschwitz and Majdanek.

Orloj Mounted on the southern wall of Old Town City Hall in the Old Town Square, the Orloj is also known as the Prague Astronomical Clock. Originally built in 1410, it has three main components: an astronomical dial, showing the position of the sun and moon in the sky and various other astronomical details; an hourly show of moving figures of the Apostles and other characters; and a calendar dial with painted circular symbols representing the months.

Orthodox Judaism The set of beliefs and practices of Jews for whom the strict observance of Jewish law is closely connected to faith; it is characterized by strict religious observance of Jewish dietary laws, restrictions on work on the Sabbath and holidays, and a modest code of dress.

partisans Members of irregular military forces or resistance movements formed to oppose armies of occupation. During World War II there were a number of different partisan groups that opposed both the Nazis and their collaborators in several countries. The term partisan could include highly organized, almost paramilitary groups such as the Red Army partisans; ad hoc groups bent more on survival than resistance; and roving groups of bandits who plundered what they could from all sides during the war.

Passover (in Hebrew, Pesach) A major festival of the Jewish calendar which takes place over eight days in the spring. One of the main observances of the holiday is to recount the story of Exodus, of the Jews' flight from slavery in Egypt, at a ritual meal called a seder. The name itself refers to the fact that God "passed over" the houses of the Jews when he set about slaying the firstborn sons of Egypt as the last of the ten plagues aimed at convincing Pharoah to free the Jews.

Prague Pankrác Remand Prison A facility used as a detention and transit camp for Jews during the Holocaust and a prison for political dissidents under the Communist regime from 1948 to 1989. Between 1943 and 1945, more than a thousand executions were carried out in the prison; under the Communists, more than 200,000 political prisoners were incarcerated there.

Rosh Hashanah (Hebrew) New Year. The autumn holiday that marks the beginning of the Jewish year and ushers in the High Holy Days. It is observed by a synagogue service that ends with blowing the *shofar* (horn), which marks the beginning of the holiday. The service is usually followed by a family dinner where traditional and symbolic foods are eaten. *See also* Yom Kippur.

shiva (Hebrew; literally, "seven") In Judaism, shiva is the seven-day mourning period that is observed after the funeral of a close relative.

Slánský, Rudolf (1901–1952) General Secretary of the Czech Communist Party from 1946 to 1951. Slánský, a Jew, had been active in the Czech Communist organization before the war, was involved in organizing the Slovak National Uprising of 1944 and, in 1946, took over the leadership of the Party. In 1951, he was suddenly ejected from the Party and, along with thirteen other Party members, ten of whom were also Jewish, he was accused of organizing a conspiracy to overthrow the government. Eleven of the accused were executed and three were given life sentences. All fourteen were officially exonerated in 1968.

Star of David (in Hebrew, *Magen David*) The six-pointed star that is the ancient and most recognizable symbol of Judaism. During World War II, Jews in Nazi-occupied areas were frequently forced to wear a badge or armband with the Star of David on it as an identifying mark of their lesser status and to single them out as targets for persecution.

United Nations Relief and Rehabilitation Administration (UNRRA) Founded in 1943 to provide assistance to victims of World War II, the organization offered food, clothing and medical necessities to both Holocaust victims and other refugees in Displaced Persons' camps.

Yom Kippur (Hebrew; literally "day of atonement") A solemn day of fasting and repentance that comes eight days after Rosh Hashanah, the Jewish New Year, and marks the end of the high holidays. *See also* Rosh Hashanah.

Zionism A movement promoted by the Viennese Jewish journalist Theodor Herzl, who argued in his 1896 book *Der Judenstaat* (The Jewish State) that the best way to resolve the problem of antisemitism and persecution of Jews in Europe was to create an independent Jewish state in the historic Jewish homeland of Biblical Israel. Zionists promoted the revival of Hebrew as a Jewish national language.

Photographs

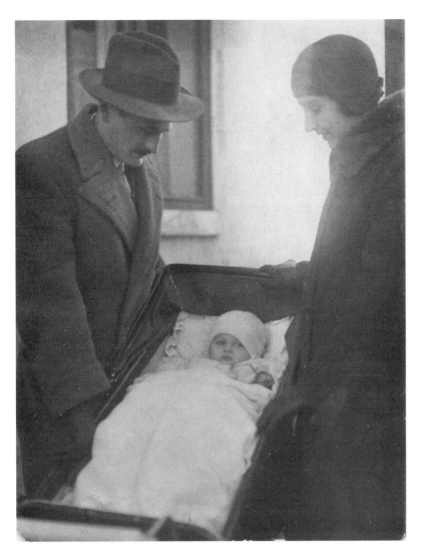

Agnes's parents, Edmund and Katka Grossmann, with Agnes, circa 1930.

1   Agnes's maternal grandparents, Zelma and Armin Kohn.

2   Agnes's parents, Edmund Grossmann and Katka Kohn, 1930.

3   Zelma Kohn (fourth from the left), and her five sisters, circa 1938.

1 Agnes at age two.

2 Agnes at age three.

3 Agnes, seven, and Ivan, three, 1937.

4 Agnes, eight, and Ivan, four, 1938.

1 Left to right: Agnes, Sarolta Neuman Grossmann (Agnes's stepmother), Ivan and Uncle Sanyi; behind: Sanyi's daughter, Katka. Bardejov Spa, circa 1935.

2 Edmund, Agnes, three, with Uncle Jozko.

3 Agnes, nine, in Bardejov during the war, 1939. Left to right: (in front) Ivan, Agnes and their father, Edmund Grossmann; (behind) Sarolta Grossmann.

1

2

1 Agnes (second row, seventh from the left) with her class in the Jewish school in Bardejov, 1941. Only seven of these children survived the Holocaust.

2 Agnes (first row, third in from the right) and her friend Magda (first row, far right) with their graduating high school class, Bardejov, 1948. Agnes and Magda are the only Jewish girls in the class.

1 Agnes and Magda, at fifteen, on the main promenade in Bardejov, 1945.

2 Agnes at sixteen years old, 1946.

3 Joe Tomasov, mid-1941, with family members, all wearing the Star of David. Left to right: Julius, Aranka, Aunt Irene, Robert and Joe.

Agnes and Joe Tomasov's wedding, Levice, August 7, 1949.

1   Agnes and Joe's wedding. Left to right: Magda, Uncle Jozko, Agnes, Joe, Sarolta, Edmund, Aunt Lotte and Uncle Sanyi.

2   Agnes and Joe on their wedding day, on the main street of Levice. Left to right: Bandi Steiner, Agnes, Joe and Uncle Jozko.

1 Left to right: Joe, Agnes and Ivan at the top of Wenceslas Square in Prague, 1950.

2 Left to right: Agnes, Joe, Sarolta, Edmund and Ivan, circa 1950.

3 Agnes and Joe's children, Tomas and Katka, 1954.

4 Agnes and Joe with Katka in Wenceslas Square in Prague, 1955.

Agnes in 1954.

1 The Tomasov family at Bardejov spa in 1955, before Joe's arrest.

2 Agnes and Tomas in 1956, during Joe's incarceration.

3 Agnes and Joe after his release from prison, 1959.

1 Ivan's graduation from medical school, Košice, 1960. Left to right: (in front) unknown, Sarolta, Edmund, Ivan, Ivan's wife, Hedika, Hedika's sister and Agnes; (behind) Uncle Sanyi, Aunt Lotte and Joe.

2 Left to right: Joe, Agnes, Hedika and Ivan, Košice, 1963.

1 Agnes with the Tomasovs' first car, the Fiat 850, in 1967.

2 Family vacation in the Low Tatra Mountains, circa 1965.

3 Left to right: (in front) Joe's uncle, Dr. Baruch Tomasov, a prominent Zionist, with Agnes and Joe; (behind) Tomas and Katka. Košice, 1966.

1 The Tomasovs with friends outside their first apartment on Eglinton Avenue in Toronto, 1969.

2 Left to right: Joe, Kathy (Katka), Agnes and Tomas outside their home in Thorn-cliffe Park, Toronto, 1969.

1 Left to right: (in front) Bandi and Jozko; (behind) Bandi's wife, Miriam, and Agnes. Kibbutz Ma'anit, Israel, 1980.

2 Edmund's first visit to Toronto, 1970. Left to right: Sarolta, Edmund, Agnes and Joe.

3 Left to right: (in front) Dr. Reichart, a friend of the family, Agnes, Sarolta and Joe; (behind) Ivan and Edmund. Toronto, 1970.

4 Left to right: Hedika, Kathy, Steve Samuel and Agnes during Ivan and Hedika's visit from Israel. Toronto, 1981.

1 Agnes with a fractured ankle. Toronto, 1974.

2 Left to right: Joe's colleague, Gordon Singer, and his girlfriend, Agnes, Kathy and Steve Samuel.

3 Kathy and Agnes at Kathy and Steve's wedding. Toronto, 1976.

4 Agnes and Joe at Kathy and Steve's wedding. Toronto, 1976.

Joe and Agnes at Agnes's mother's grave during their first trip to Czechoslovakia since their defection. Košice, 1991.

Four generations of the Kohn-Tomasov women: Agnes's grandmother Zelma Kohn at the top and left to right: Kathy, her daughter, Daniella, and Agnes. 1979.

Joe and Agnes Tomasov on their 60th wedding anniversary, 2009.

Index

Mount Sinai Hospital, 136, 138
Muller, Mrs., 128
Nazi Germany, xiii–xv, xvii
Neuman, Elisabeth, 6, 10
Neuman, Irene, 6, 10
Neuman, Miklos, 6, 13
Neuman, Sarolta (Agnes's step-
 mother). See Grossmann,
 Sarolta.
Neuman, Mrs. (Sarolta's mother),
 10, 13, 15, 17–18, 23, 31, 33, 35, 43,
 45–47, 99–100
Neumann, Julish, 56, 135
Neumann, Magda, 9, 11, 33, 35, 37,
 40, 49, 56, 58, 60, 67–68, 83, 135
Novak, Lilly, 128, 134
Nováky labour camp (Slovakia), 12,
 54, 58
Novotný, Antonín, xxii, 116n2, 117n3
Nuremberg Laws, xiv–xvi
Nyköping (Sweden), 119
Ondrušková, 2
Orava (Slovakia), 52–53, 57
Orloj (Prague), 75, 155
Otto (Joe's cousin), 135
Palestine, 8, 53. See also Israel.
Pankrác Remand Prison (Prague),
 91
partisans, xvii, 17–18, 19, 21–22,
 24–26, 54. See also Jewish
 partisans.
Pesach (Passover), 144–145
Pista (cousin in Budapest), 139, 140,
 141
Poland, xiii–xiv, xxiii–xxiv, 12, 14

Poprad (Slovakia), 30
Prague, 1, 42–43, 45, 57, 58, 59, 60,
 61, 87, 92, 107, 119, 145n3, 146
Prague Spring, xxiii–xxiv, xxvii,
 117n3, 119n4
Prešov (Slovakia), 2, 6, 10, 30, 47
Quittner family, 54
Raslavice (Slovakia), 30
Red Army, xvii–xviii, 14, 21, 21n3,
 27, 30, 54
Red Cross, 29
Reichard, Dr., 112
Reitmann, Imre and Magda, 136
Rigor, Paul, 136
Romankova, Viola, 122
Rosh Hashanah, 144
Ružomberok (Slovakia), 22
Samuel, Anyuci, 134–135, 143–144
Samuel, Daniella, 136–138
Samuel, Kathy. See Tomasov, Katka.
Samuel, Jonathan, 138
Samuel, Elliott, 142
Samuel, Michelle, 142
Samuel, Ocsi, 134–135, 143
Samuel, Oded, 134, 135
Samuel, Steven, 133–135, 137, 138
Schuster, Professor, 102
Schweitzer, Dr. Arpad, 99
Schwejcar, Dr., 68
Sered labour camp (Slovakia), 12
Shaarei Shomayim synagogue
 (Toronto), 135
Siegel, Dr., 88, 107
Simkova, Anna, 11
Sinai War, Israel (1956), xx

The Azrieli Foundation was established in 1989 to realize and extend the philanthropic vision of David J. Azrieli, C.M., C.Q., M.Arch. The Foundation's mission is to support a wide spectrum of initiatives in education and research. The Azrieli Foundation is an active supporter of programs in the fields of Jewish education, the education of architects, scientific and medical research, and education in the arts. The Azrieli Foundation's many well-known initiatives include: the Holocaust Survivor Memoirs Program, which collects, preserves, publishes and distributes the written memoirs of survivors in Canada; the Azrieli Institute for Educational Empowerment, an innovative program successfully working to keep at-risk youth in school; and the Azrieli Fellows Program, which promotes academic excellence and leadership on the graduate level at Israeli universities.

MURDER
ON THE
LAKE OF FIRE

MIKEL J. WILSON

MOURNING DOVE MYSTERIES: MURDER ON THE LAKE
OF FIRE

Cover design by Damonza.com.

Author portrait by Dave Meyer at DaveMeyerDesign.com.

Mikel J. Wilson
555 W. Country Club Lane, C-222
Escondido, CA 92026

MikelJWilson.com

Paperback ISBN: 978-1-947392-06-9
Hardcover ISBN: 978-1-947392-07-6

First Edition, December 2017

Printed in the United States of America through Acorn Publishing at
AcornPublishingLLC.com.